Go Roth!

Your guide to the
Roth IRA and
other Roth accounts

2015 Edition
Kaye A. Thomas

Go Roth!

Your Guide to the Roth IRA and Other Roth Accounts

2015 Edition

This printing of *Go Roth!* reflects relevant legal authorities as of January 15, 2015.

Fairmark Press Inc.
www.fairmark.com
(630) 728-3835

Print edition ISBN-13: 978-1-938797-06-4

Printed in the United States of America

Table of Contents

Part I: What Hath Roth Wrought 9

1 Roth to the Rescue 11

2 Life Cycle of a Roth Account 17

Part II: To Roth or Not to Roth 25

3 Imagine 27

4 The Tax Savings Preservation Fallacy 31

5 The Parity Principle 35

6 Size Matters 38

7 The Fourth Dimension 41

8 Rate Shifting 44

9 IRA vs. Employer Account 52

10 The Conversion Decision 59

11 Saving for Other Goals 66

Part III: Contributions to Roth Accounts 73

12 How to Start a Roth IRA 75

13 Roth IRA Contributions 81

14 Qualifying Income for IRA Contributions 88

15 Income Limitation for Roth IRA Contributions 97

16 Backdoor Roth IRA Contributions 103

17 Roth Accounts in 401k and Similar Plans 109

18 Retirement Savings Contributions Credit 115

19 Retroactive Switching 120

20 Troubleshooting Contributions 129

Part IV: Roth Conversions 141

21 Roth Conversions 143

22 Conversion Consequences 155

23 Recharacterizing Conversions 163
24 Conversion Strategy Fundamentals 175
25 Advanced Conversion Strategies 185

Part V: Managing Your Account 195

26 Tax Rules for IRA Investments 197
27 Investing Your Retirement Account 206
28 Rollovers and Direct Transfers 234

Part VI: Taking Money Out 253

29 Distribution Overview 255
30 Five-Year Test 260
31 Exceptions to Age 59½ Test 268
32 Nonqualified Distributions 274
33 Liquidating an Account for a Loss 291
34 Inherited Roth Account 295

Index 301

About the Author

After many years as a lawyer dealing with tax matters relating to business transactions, finance and compensation, Kaye Thomas now spends most of his time as a writer, publisher, public speaker and consultant on topics relating to taxation and investments. Kaye also maintains a free web site called *Tax Guide for Investors* at Fairmark.com, providing hundreds of pages of plain language tax guidance and featuring a message board where Kaye and others respond to questions and comments from readers.

Kaye's law degree is from Harvard Law School, where he served on the *Harvard Law Review* and graduated *cum laude* in 1980.

Also by the Author

That Thing Rich People Do
The shortest, easiest way to learn what everyone needs to know about investing.

Capital Gains, Minimal Taxes
A guide for people who buy and sell stock, mutual funds and stock options.

Consider Your Options
The leading book on how to handle stock options and other forms of equity compensation.

Equity Compensation Strategies
A text for professionals who offer advice on stock options and other forms of equity compensation.

Visit Fairmark.com for details.

About This Edition

This is the fourth edition of *Go Roth!*, bringing it up to date through January 15, 2015. We've made changes throughout the book reflecting new tax rates, inflation adjustments and similar routine matters. Since the previous edition, we also have some significant new developments.

We previously had the ability to convert a 401k or similar account to a Roth account within the same plan, but limitations on this opportunity closed it off from many people. The new rules still require action from employers to make in-plan conversions possible, but the opportunity has been expanded to make it more generally available. See Chapter 21.

For those who have made (or plan to make) after-tax contributions to a regular (non-Roth) account in a 401k or similar plan, a new interpretation by the IRS makes it easier than in the past to isolate basis when taking a distribution. This means that if you're eligible to withdraw from such an account, you can make a tax-free rollover of the pre-tax dollars and a zero-tax conversion of the after-tax dollars. See Chapter 25.

Another new interpretation, prompted by a court decision, gives us a stricter version of the rule limiting us to one IRA rollover per year. Previously the IRS told us it was okay to have more than one rollover in the same year provided that each rollover involved different IRAs for both the source and destination. Now it's one and done: wait twelve months before doing another rollover (although you can still do trustee-to-trustee transfers without regard to this rule). See Chapter 28.

Some practitioners—a small minority, we believe—have raised the question whether the IRS might mount a challenge to the "backdoor Roth contribution" strategy. We've added a discussion of this issue in Chapter 16. Spoiler alert: we see no cause for concern.

Similarly, we take note of, but don't believe there is need to worry about, a proposal to make the minimum required distribution rules apply to the original owner of a Roth IRA. See Chapter 7.

Part I
What Hath Roth Wrought

1 Roth to the Rescue

2 Life Cycle of a Roth Account

1

Roth to the Rescue

A Roth account can help meet the retirement challenges of the twenty-first century.

THEY SAY ONLY DEATH AND TAXES are certain, but you can avoid one of them. Using a Roth IRA, or a Roth account in a 401k or similar plan, you can grow your retirement wealth tax-free.

Traditional retirement accounts allow you to *delay* paying tax, often for many years. That helps the account grow faster, but you'll have taxable income later when you withdraw the money. The more the account grows, the more tax you end up paying. The IRS is a silent partner sharing in your success.

In a Roth account, all the money is working for you. Follow the rules and you'll never pay income tax on the earnings. It's like having a tax haven, except you don't have to deal with a shady outfit that operates out of a post office box on a tropical island.

Opening the door

The Roth revolution began in 1998 with the introduction of the Roth IRA, named for a senator who pushed for its creation. Changes over the years have made these accounts available to more people.

- *2005.* Conversions become easier with a change in the way the income limitation was calculated.
- *2006.* Income limits for contributions to Roth IRAs are indexed for inflation.
- *2006.* Employers are permitted to offer Roth accounts in 401k and 403b plans.
- *2008.* Direct conversions are permitted, where money goes from a traditional account in an employer plan directly into a Roth IRA.
- *2010.* The $100,000 income limitation on Roth conversions disappears.
- *2010.* Employers can offer "in-plan" conversions, moving money from a traditional 401k account to a Roth account in the same plan.
- *2011.* State and local governments can offer Roth accounts in 457b plans.
- *2012.* The federal government's huge Thrift Savings Plan begins offering Roth accounts.
- *2013.* The rules for "in-plan" conversions are relaxed, making it possible for employers to offer this option more broadly.
- *2014.* A changed interpretation by the IRS makes it easier to isolate after-tax dollars for a tax-free conversion when taking money from a 401k or similar plan.

Two Roths make a right. Especially significant is the availability of Roth accounts in 401k and similar plans. These accounts are not exactly the same as Roth IRAs, but they work on the same basic principle. If your company offers this option, you can enter the tax-free world of Roth retirement savings without giving up matching contributions or other advantages of saving in an employer plan.

> In this book, the term *Roth account* includes all these accounts: the Roth IRA plus Roth accounts in employer plans. When necessary we'll refer to the Roth IRA or employer accounts separately.

A timely benefit

The Roth revolution comes at a time of profound change in retirement planning. Several megatrends are converging to shift responsibility for retirement security away from government and employers and onto the shoulders of individual retirees.

Longer retirements. People are living longer. Life expectancy in the United States was less than 70 years as recently as 1960. Now it's close to 80 years. That figure represents life expectancy at birth, an average that includes members of the population that die young. The life expectancy of someone who survives to age 65 stretches to age 85 or so. Of course that's an average too, so you have to be prepared for the possibility of a retirement that may extend for decades.

Baby boomers. Birth rates increased dramatically following World War II and remained high for a number of years before leveling off and falling. The result is an unusually large generation, often called *baby boomers.* The earliest boomers turned 60 in 2006. The aging and retirement of the baby boom generation will have major implications for various government programs and for the economy in general.

Demise of pensions. American businesses are in the midst of a massive shift away from pension plans that provide payments based on years of service (called *defined benefit plans*) to 401k plans and others that provide benefits based on the size of your account balance (called *defined contribution plans*). Defined benefit plans require the employer to set aside money in a pension fund based on educated guesses about how well the investments will perform and how long the beneficiaries will live. These plans are expensive to maintain and expose the company to the risk that they'll have to pony up extra money if the fund falls short. Companies in all sectors of the economy are phasing out traditional pensions.

Account-based plans like the 401k are simpler and less expensive for companies to maintain. These plans also offer advantages to workers in a mobile workforce because the benefits are more portable. Yet the move from defined benefit to defined contribution plans also means you can work many years without building a secure source of income for retirement if you save too little or manage your account poorly.

Social Security. When we published the first edition of this book in 2008, projections indicated the Social Security program would continue to collect more in taxes than it pays out in benefits through 2015, and that reserves built up over the years would permit the Social Security Administration to continue paying full benefits until 2041. Those projections didn't anticipate the Great Recession. Higher unemployment reduced the amount of Social Security tax collected by the government. At the same time, many boomers began claiming benefits earlier than they might have in a stronger economy. As a result, the first year with benefits exceeding tax revenues arrived in 2010, and the most recent (2014) annual report of the Social Security Trustees projects that unless Congress acts to shore up the system, the Social Security trust fund will be exhausted in 2033.

> At that point the program would not stop running, but it would be forced to reduce benefits. The SSA estimates that benefits would be cut by about 25%, a result that would be painful for many recipients and disastrous for some.

No one expects Congress to sit by for decades while this train wreck unfolds. On the other hand our politicians aren't exactly eager to confront this problem, because a solution will almost surely require some combination of tax increases and benefit cuts, both of which are unpopular. Social Security will survive, but it's likely to become less generous.

Not a toy on a string. The world in which many workers could rely on a company pension and generous Social Security payments for a comfortable retirement is giving way to a new reality called *YOYO* retirement: *You're On Your Own.* Your financial security is going to depend on the choices you make. You need to be smart about how much to save, how to invest, when to draw money from your account—and the type of account you use.

Roth to the rescue

Roth accounts don't solve all these problems, but they can help meet the challenges of YOYO retirement. They offer four main advantages over traditional retirement accounts.

First and foremost is the chance to make your investment earnings *permanently tax-free.* This advantage by itself is often equal to or greater than the benefit of claiming a deduction when you contribute to a traditional retirement account. Second, a Roth account is effectively larger than a traditional retirement account, because all the money is working for you. The IRS doesn't get to share in your success. Third, the minimum distribution rules that apply to traditional IRAs beginning at age 70½ don't apply to Roth IRAs. In fact, you can continue making contributions to a Roth IRA after age 70½ if you have qualifying income. That means the tax benefits of Roth accounts can be preserved far longer. And fourth, Roth IRA owners can usually withdraw at least some of their money before age 59½ without paying a penalty tax.

Overall, Roth accounts make it easier to build, preserve and use your retirement savings. We'll expand on these points in Part II.

2

Life Cycle of a Roth Account

Here's an overview of rules governing the creation, maintenance and use of Roth accounts.

THIS BOOK IS BUILT AROUND the life cycle of a Roth account. Part II deals with the choice you have to make at the outset, to use a Roth account or a traditional account. Parts III (contributions) and IV (conversions) cover all you need to know about getting money into the account. Part V deals with issues that come up in managing a Roth account: investments and rollovers. Finally, we talk about taking money out—distributions—in Part VI.

There's a lot to learn, and you need at least a general outline of the rules covered in the later parts of the book to appreciate the benefits of Roth accounts discussed in Part II. This chapter provides the overview you need to get started.

Contributions

When you put money in a regular bank account you make a *deposit.* A deposit to a retirement account is called a *contribution.* Different word, but exactly the same thing.

Contributions to Roth accounts don't produce deductions. That means the amount of income you report, and the amount of tax you pay, won't change as a result of your contributions. Here are the main rules for contributions.

Roth IRAs. Some of the rules for contributions to Roth IRAs are the same as for traditional IRAs. In both cases, for example, your contribution for any year can be made any time from January 1 of that year until April 15 of the following year. The dollar limitation is the same, too. If you're under 50 years of age, your contributions can be as much as $5,500. (This limit applies as of 2015; the limit for subsequent years will depend on inflation adjustments.) If you're 50 or older by the end of the year, you can add another $1,000. This is an overall dollar limit for contributions to both types of IRA. If you contribute to a traditional IRA for the same year, your Roth contribution limit is reduced by that amount. You also need to have compensation or alimony income (or rely on your spouse having such income) at least equal to the amount of your contribution.

There are two special requirements for Roth IRA contributions. First, if you're married, you have to file jointly. (It's theoretically possible to contribute while married filing separately but as a practical matter hardly anyone can do this.) And second, your modified adjusted gross income can't exceed certain limits, which are adjusted each year for inflation. For the maximum contribution, the limits for 2015 are $116,000 for single individuals and $183,000 for married individuals filing joint returns. The amount you can contribute is reduced gradually and then completely eliminated when income exceeds those amounts.

> You can contribute to a Roth IRA even if you participate in a 401k or other employer retirement plan.

Roth accounts in employer plans. Roth accounts are now allowed in 401k and similar plans, although employers are not required to offer this alternative. You can contribute if you work for an employer that offers these accounts and you meet the requirements to participate in the plan. These contributions are subject to the same limits that apply when you contribute to a traditional account in the same employer plan. Here again, these limits apply to your total contributions to both traditional and Roth accounts, so any amount you contribute to a traditional account in a given year reduces the amount you can contribute to a Roth account for the same year.

> Not all employers offer Roth accounts in their retirement plans, but this alternative is quite common and is coming to be seen as a standard feature of these plans.

Conversions

If you have a traditional IRA you can convert some or all of that IRA into a Roth IRA. (Prior to 2010 conversions were not permitted if you were married filing separately or if your income was above $100,000.) When you do this, you have to pay tax on the amount converted based on the current value of the assets.

We now have three possible ways to convert a traditional account in an employer plan to a Roth account. (All require you to be eligible to withdraw from the account.) You can roll the account to a traditional IRA and then do an IRA conversion; you can convert directly from the employer account to a Roth IRA; or, if your employer permits, you can convert *within* the employer plan, so you have a Roth account in that plan instead of a Roth IRA.

Recharacterizations

That's a huge word for an important set of rules you can use to correct various problems with Roth IRAs. The basic idea is to change something that happened in the past if it turned out to be a mistake. When it's available, a recharacterization provides what golfers call a mulligan, a chance to do over something that didn't turn out right.

> **Example:** Suppose you converted a traditional IRA to a Roth but later decided the conversion wasn't a good idea. These rules allow you to undo the conversion and act as if it never happened.

You can even use recharacterizations to change an annual contribution from one type of IRA to another (traditional to Roth or vice versa). This is a powerful tool that has gotten many people out of a jam. Generally you have to act by October 15 of the year after the one you're trying to fix.

Investments

Normally you have a fair amount of choice as to how the money in your retirement account is invested. You make an initial choice at the time you set up the account and you can make changes later.

Employers usually offer a specific menu of investment choices for 401k plans. You simply choose the amount you want to go into each of those choices. An IRA can offer wider choices. In fact, your IRA can make just about any kind of investment, but there are a few restrictions. The tax law has a list of types of investments you aren't allowed to make with an IRA, such as artwork, antiques, and certain "collectibles." Also, you can't use an IRA for an investment that involves "self-dealing," such as the purchase of a home in which you or a relative will reside.

Rollovers

The rollover rules allow you to move retirement savings from one account to another.

From employer accounts. Although some plans permit "in-service withdrawals," generally you can't move your money from a 401k or similar account until you stop working for that employer. At that point you can roll it over to a new employer's retirement plan or to an IRA. A traditional account can move to another traditional account (an IRA or an account with your new employer) and, as noted above, can now be converted directly to a Roth IRA. You can roll a Roth 401k or similar account to a Roth account with your new employer or to a Roth IRA. Generally it's best to set up your rollover as a *direct transfer* to avoid withholding and other potential problems.

> A direct transfer moves cash or other account assets directly from one trustee to another.

From IRAs. You can move money from one IRA to another using either a rollover or a direct transfer. You can do a direct transfer at any time, but rollovers are permitted only once within a twelve-month period.

Distributions from Roth IRAs

Distributions from a Roth IRA can be entirely tax-free, but only if you follow certain rules. For most people this means meeting two requirements: you've had a Roth IRA at least five years, and you're over 59½ at the time of the distribution. There are special rules for disability and death, and for first-time homebuyers.

Early distributions. If you need to take money from your Roth IRA before age 59½, you can withdraw your contributions (other than from conversions) at any time without paying tax or penalty. After withdrawing your contributions, you can withdraw the amount of any conversions. These withdrawals are tax-free (you already paid tax on these amounts at the time of the conversion) but you may pay a 10% penalty if you're under 59½ and the conversion was within the last five years. A nonqualified distribution of investment earnings that built up in the Roth account is taxable and can be hit with the 10% penalty as well.

Required distributions. When you have a traditional IRA, you have to take required minimum distributions (*RMDs*) beginning with the year you turn 70½. This rule doesn't apply to Roth IRAs, so if you can meet your living expenses from other resources, you can preserve your Roth IRA, continuing to build up tax-free investment earnings. Distributions from a Roth IRA are required only after the death of the owner.

Distributions from employer plan Roth accounts

Unless the plan allows in-service withdrawals, you can't take money from a 401k or similar account while you're still working for the employer that maintains the plan. The requirements for tax-free distributions from a Roth account in an employer plan are roughly the same as for a Roth IRA: you need to have your Roth account at least five years and be over 59½. Unlike a Roth IRA, the time you've had one account won't necessarily count toward the time you need to hold another account.

Early distributions. If you take an early distribution from a Roth account in an employer plan, the part representing a return of your contributions is free of tax or penalty. You don't get to take your contributions first, though. The distribution will be allocated between earnings and a return of contributions, so you may have to pay some tax and early distribution penalty before you've withdrawn all your contributions.

Required distributions. The Roth IRA enjoys an exemption from the rule that requires minimum distributions beginning at age 70½, but Roth accounts in employer plans do not. There's an easy solution if you want to preserve your account, however: you can roll your employer account to a Roth IRA before you reach the age when minimum distributions are required. After that you'll be free to leave the money in the account as long as you want.

Part II
To Roth or Not to Roth

3 Imagine

4 The Tax Savings Preservation Fallacy

5 The Parity Principle

6 Size Matters

7 The Fourth Dimension

8 Rate Shifting

9 IRA vs. Employer Account

10 The Conversion Decision

11 Saving for Other Goals

3

Imagine

Project yourself into the future and ask which would you rather have: a traditional account or a Roth.

LET'S BEGIN HERE. Before we get into the details of how one type of retirement account might outperform another, imagine what life might be like when you're ready to tap your retirement account, and consider which type you'd rather have.

Your golden years

We're talking about a retirement account, so it makes sense to begin by looking at its use during retirement.

Traditional. If you've built your nest egg in a traditional account, every withdrawal will be taxable income. Unless your overall income is below the threshold where tax applies, a portion of each payment has to be set aside for Uncle Sam.

What's more, these withdrawals can affect your other retirement benefits. A change in your overall level of income, including income from retirement plan distributions, can affect the amount of tax you pay on your Social Security benefits. Medicare premiums may also be adjusted based on your income level: you pay more when your income rises above certain (relatively high) thresholds, and that includes money you draw from a traditional retirement account.

To make matters worse, you don't have complete freedom concerning the scheduling of payments from these accounts. Once you reach age 70½ you're required to pull a minimum amount from the account each year, even if you don't need the money.

> The minimum distribution rules make it harder for you to pass a traditional retirement account to your loved ones—and they'll have to pay tax on distributions from whatever portion of the account you're able to preserve for them.

Roth. The picture is quite different when you retire with a Roth account. If you follow all the rules, every dollar you withdraw is free of income tax. It's all spendable. Compared with a traditional account of the same size, a Roth offers a more comfortable retirement.

Social Security? No worries. Nontaxable Roth distributions don't count in determining how much of this benefit is taxable. These distributions don't affect your Medicare premiums, either.

What about those required minimum distribution rules that kick in at age 70½? They don't apply to Roth IRAs. They *do* apply to Roth accounts in retirement plans, but that won't matter if you roll the employer account into a Roth IRA.

If you find that you don't need to draw from this account during retirement you can leave it intact for your beneficiaries—and they won't pay any tax when they withdraw the money.

Tapping the account early

Now let's imagine another possibility. Life doesn't always work out the way we plan, and it happens all too often that people need to draw from their retirement savings before they retire. A period of unemployment or some other emergency may lead them to dip into an IRA or take a hardship distribution from the retirement plan where they work.

Traditional. Here again, amounts drawn from a traditional account are generally taxable. There are a couple of ugly twists, though. This is happening before you retired, so the income may fall in a year when you're still earning, and haven't yet moved to the lower tax bracket you anticipate in retirement.

What's worse, if this happens before you reach age 59½, you could be hit with an additional 10% penalty tax for taking an early distribution from your retirement savings. There are exceptions to this penalty that may prevent it from applying in certain types of emergencies, such as when you have heavy medical expenses. The law doesn't provide a generalized hardship exception, though, so many people get hit with this penalty at the worst possible time. When you take state income tax into account as well, you may not be able to spend much more than half of the amount you withdraw.

Roth. No problemo. Not nearly as much of one, anyway. No matter when you pull money from the account, the portion treated as coming from your contributions will be free of tax and also free of the 10% penalty tax on early distributions. Income tax and that nasty early withdrawal penalty can apply to the portion that's treated as coming from investment earnings of the account, but normally this is a small fraction, if any, of the amount withdrawn.

What this tells us

When it comes time to use your retirement account, you'd rather have a Roth. This is true whether you have to tap it early, or use it during retirement, or end up passing it on to beneficiaries.

That isn't the whole story, of course. Traditional accounts can provide you with a deduction in the year you contribute to the account, and you forgo that deduction when you go Roth. The benefit of that deduction can outweigh the benefits you anticipate from a Roth account. Then again . . .

4

The Tax Savings Preservation Fallacy

There's a fundamental mistake underlying much of the analysis used to choose between traditional and Roth accounts.

BEFORE WE GET INTO MORE DETAILED ANALYSIS we need to understand why many people, including qualified experts, go wrong in thinking about the choice between saving in a traditional account or a Roth. I call it the *tax savings preservation fallacy*, or *TSPF*. It's very simple yet commonly overlooked and profoundly important.

The goal: spendable dollars

When you think about it, our main goal is to maximize the number of spendable dollars you'll have in retirement. Expert analysis will often churn through numbers to determine whether the deduction you receive for contributing to a traditional account boosts this number more than the back-end benefit of a Roth account, the ability to withdraw money tax-free. The typical conclusion is that a traditional account is likely to provide a richer retirement than a Roth if you're in a higher tax bracket when you contribute to the account than when you take the money out.

Although there's some merit to this analysis, we're going to see that there are ways a Roth account can overcome a tax bracket disadvantage. Before we get to that point, though, we should understand that there's a questionable assumption underlying all the number crunching. This chapter exists to challenge that assumption.

The fallacy

Here it is: almost all comparisons between traditional and Roth retirement accounts proceed on the assumption that the tax savings achieved by deducting a contribution to a traditional account ends up being preserved as part of your retirement savings. I'm not aware of any study of this proposition, but I believe it's more false than true.

Consider this scenario. Kevin is planning to contribute $250 per month to a retirement plan, or $3,000 for the year. If he's in the 25% tax bracket, the deduction he gets for contributing this money to a traditional account will reduce his income tax by $750. He won't get this deduction if he chooses a Roth, so a typical analysis of Kevin's situation will begin with the notion that his choice is between saving $3,000 in a traditional account or $2,250 in a Roth. Then we look at how the money grows over the years and consider the tax impact when Kevin uses the account in retirement.

That's how the analysis goes, but it isn't how things work in the real world. Kevin isn't actually choosing between putting $3,000 in a traditional account or $2,250 in a Roth. He's planning to save $3,000, and deciding which type of account to use for that amount of savings. It might be more logical to compare differing amounts of savings that take the tax benefit into account, but Kevin is a human, not a computer, and he's just thinking about where to save $3,000.

What happens when he saves in a traditional account? If it's a 401k, the contribution reduces his taxable wages, and the company reduces the amount of income tax withholding. Kevin's take-home pay is about $15 per week more than if he saved in a Roth. Chances are he doesn't even notice the difference, and it disappears into the purchase of a few more lattes. They taste good going down, but don't add much to his quality of life. Meanwhile he's saddled with the deferred tax liability of a traditional retirement account. *The money saved by claiming a deduction has not been preserved.*

Things might work out a little differently if he saves in an IRA, because this choice won't affect the amount of income tax withheld from his paycheck. The $3,000 deduction may enable him to receive the entire $750 tax benefit at one time, in the form of an income tax refund. He has a better chance of preserving this amount than when it comes in dribs and drabs, $15 per week. But I'm betting he spends it on a new iPad.

Now look what happens if he puts the $3,000 in a Roth instead. The money is all there, and it's all his. As we saw in the previous chapter, this account will be more valuable to him, regardless of whether he retains it until retirement or makes an emergency withdrawal earlier in life. He's given up those lattes, or he may have to use his older iPad for a little longer. The thing he hasn't done, though, is give up the tax benefit associated with saving in a retirement account. In a Roth, that benefit comes at the end, when the money comes out, so it doesn't disappear in spending choices made earlier. Kevin ends up with a more valuable retirement account if he decides to go Roth.

Theory and practice

I'm not saying the benefit of the tax deduction should be disregarded. A comparison between Roth and traditional accounts that takes this up-front benefit into account is a useful exercise, one we'll discuss in the chapters ahead. We shouldn't treat that analysis as conclusive proof that one type of account will produce better results, though. Best in theory isn't always best in practice. Many people will do better with a Roth even if the math points to a traditional account.

5

The Parity Principle

Comparisons between traditional and Roth accounts revolve around the *parity principle*.

NOW WE'RE READY TO ROLL UP OUR SLEEVES and do some analysis. Roth accounts are likely to work out better than traditional accounts for most people. The first step in seeing why is to understand something I call the *parity principle*. It tells us that under certain conditions, both types of accounts produce exactly the same results. When we change those conditions, we see how one type can gain an advantage.

Side by side

Suppose you divide your savings between a traditional account and a Roth. You put $2,000 into a traditional account. You're in the 25% bracket, so this contribution produces $500 in tax savings, for an after-tax cost of $1,500. Keeping the after-tax cost the same, you put $1,500 into a Roth. You make the same investments in both accounts and wait to see what happens.

The money remains invested long enough to triple in value. The Roth ends up with $4,500 you can withdraw tax-free. Your traditional account has $6,000, but if you're still in the 25% bracket you'll pay $1,500 of income tax when you take the money out. That leaves you with $4,500, exactly the same amount produced by the Roth. The two accounts produce the same amount of spendable wealth.

This result isn't a coincidence. It follows from a simple rule of math: the result of multiplying *A* times *B* is the same as *B* times *A*. In this case, *A* is 300%, the multiplier produced by investment growth, and *B* is 75%, the amount of money left after paying the 25% income tax. In the traditional account we multiply *A* times *B*, putting investment growth ahead of taxes. In the Roth we apply the tax factor first and then get the investment growth. When both accounts enjoy the same investment growth and bear the same tax burden, they produce the same result. That's the *parity principle.*

> The parity principle says that other things being equal, tax deferral and tax-free investing produce the same result. Except when something disturbs the parity principle, the Roth and the traditional account are two different paths to the same destination.

What we assumed

We had to make some assumptions to arrive at this perfectly equal result. Let's spell them out.

- You contributed more money to the traditional account than the Roth ($2,000 versus $1,500 in our example). This is a key point in the comparison, potentially providing a huge advantage to the Roth, because contribution limits are generally the same for both types of accounts.

- Both accounts produced the same investment performance. That's a fair enough assumption, because you can make the same types of investments in both kinds of accounts.
- You pulled money out of both accounts at the same time. This is another potential advantage for the Roth, because the minimum distribution rules that apply to traditional IRAs don't apply to Roth IRAs.
- Your tax rate was the same in retirement as in the years you contributed to your account. This factor can favor either kind of account, depending on your situation.

In the following chapters we'll examine what happens when we change these assumptions. Most of the changes will favor Roth accounts over traditional accounts.

6

Size Matters

To produce the same benefit, a traditional account has to be larger than a Roth.

OUR FIRST LOOK AT THE PARITY PRINCIPLE showed that a $1,500 Roth contribution can produce the same end result as a $2,000 contribution to a traditional account. Let's focus on that fact for a moment. *To produce the same result, the traditional account has to be 33% larger than the Roth.*

Here's another way to look at the same relationship. *If both accounts are the same size, the Roth will produce 33% more spendable wealth in retirement.* That's a stunning difference in results. This is the main reason most people should choose Roth accounts for their retirement savings.

Tax brackets

The difference in the effective size of the two accounts depends on your tax bracket in retirement, but the effect is greater than the percentages used as tax rates. In the 15% tax bracket a Roth provides nearly 18% more spendable wealth than a traditional account of the same size. We saw above that the 25% bracket translates into a 33% difference. If withdrawals would be taxed at 39.6%, the difference balloons to 65%. When you consider state income taxes—or the possibility that federal tax rates will rise—the difference can be even greater.

TSPF revisited

This is where the rubber meets the road for the tax savings preservation fallacy, discussed in Chapter 4. In many cases it's possible to avoid this difference in spendable wealth by adding more money to the traditional account than the Roth. In theory you have the means to do this, because the more or less immediate tax savings you get from contributing to a traditional account frees up money for *additional* savings. If you're the kind of person who will check to see that your tax bracket is 25% and then weigh the difference between $2,000 of savings in a traditional account and $1,500 of savings in a Roth, you may be able to cancel out the back-end advantage of the Roth. It's my contention that people who think this way are a rare breed.

In any event, there are situations where it simply isn't possible to boost a traditional account to the level that would make it equivalent to a Roth, as discussed next.

Contribution limits

Most of the limits that apply to Roth contributions are the same as the limits that apply to traditional accounts. If you're able to max out your contributions to a Roth account, there's no way to boost your traditional account to the higher level that would provide equivalent value in retirement.

True, you can set aside additional savings in a regular, taxable investment account. There's no reason to view the limits on retirement account contributions as a limit on your overall savings. Yet savings outside your retirement account won't grow as fast because they aren't sheltered from taxation. The importance of this issue depends on various factors, including your tax bracket and investment style.

> The key point: contribution limits may prevent you from creating as much wealth in a traditional account as you can create in a Roth.

Conversions

Another place where the size differential comes into play is when converting a traditional account to a Roth. If you can pay the tax cost of a conversion without drawing money from your retirement account, you've increased the number of dollars sheltered from tax. Here again, a Roth account offers a potential increase in overall retirement savings that isn't available in a traditional account.

> Chapter 10 discusses the conversion decision.

7

The Fourth Dimension

Roth accounts can be preserved longer than traditional accounts.

IN THE PREVIOUS CHAPTER WE SAW that a Roth can be bigger than a traditional retirement account. It can also extend farther in the fourth dimension: time.

Required minimum distributions

The rules for traditional accounts require you to pull money out of the account beginning at age 70½. You're forced to reduce the size of this tax-advantaged account—and to add taxable income to your tax return—even if you don't need the money at that time.

The minimum distribution rules don't apply to the original owner of a Roth IRA. Distributions are required for an inherited Roth IRA if the beneficiary is someone other than the spouse of the original owner. During your lifetime though, if you can meet your financial needs from other resources you can preserve the account as long as you want, perhaps even leaving the entire amount to your heirs. The result can be years or even decades of continued tax-free growth.

> The minimum distribution rules *do* apply to Roth accounts in employer plans, but there's a simple way to deal with that problem: roll the account to a Roth IRA at the appropriate time.

If retirement is a long way off, it may be hard for you to imagine being over 70 and still wanting to preserve your retirement account. Trust me on this: there are plenty of people who feel the pinch from the minimum distribution rules. Avoiding that requirement can make a difference in the amount of wealth you have for your later years, or the amount you can pass to beneficiaries.

Obama proposal. President Obama's official wish list for tax changes (known in the trade as the *Greenbook*) includes altered minimum distribution rules. Their scope would be expanded to apply to Roth IRAs, but at the same time, people with less than $100,000 in retirement savings would be exempted altogether. With some exceptions, non-spouse beneficiaries would be required to empty an inherited account by the end of the fifth year after the year the account owner died. The changes would apply to individuals who attain age 70½ after 2014.

> No groundswell of support for this proposal is apparent. While we can't exclude the possibility it will become law, at the writing the likelihood appears to be small.

Effect on other benefits

The steady stream of taxable income you're required to take from a traditional IRA can impose an added cost in retirement because of the way Social Security benefits are taxed. When your income is below a given threshold, you don't pay tax on Social Security benefits. As your income rises above that level, the portion of your Social Security benefit that's taxed gradually increases, up to 85%. Many people find themselves with income in the range where required minimum distributions from traditional retirement accounts are causing them to pay tax on a greater portion of their Social Security.

You eliminate that problem if you have a Roth account. The minimum distribution rules don't apply to a Roth IRA. What's more, you won't have this problem even if you *are* taking regular distributions from a Roth. These distributions aren't included in income, so they don't affect the amount of tax you pay on your Social Security benefits.

> Tax-exempt interest is taken into account in determining how much of your Social Security benefit is taxable, but tax-exempt Roth distributions are not.

Medicare premiums. Taxation of Social Security benefits kicks in at relatively modest levels of income. If your income is quite a bit higher, so that you know you'll pay tax on those benefits in any event, you may have to deal with a different issue. The premiums you pay for Medicare coverage increase when your income exceeds certain thresholds. Having a Roth account instead of a traditional retirement account can help keep your income below those levels.

8

Rate Shifting

This is one variation from the parity principle that can favor either type of retirement account.

THE PERFECTLY EQUAL OUTCOMES produced by the parity principle require us to assume your tax rate in retirement will be the same as in the years you contribute to your account. Let's see what happens when we change that assumption.

The relevant rate

Before we talk about changing tax rates, we have to know what rates we're talking about. For this purpose, the rate that matters is your *marginal* income tax rate. That's not the same as the average rate that applies to your income, and it's not the same as the rate of withholding you see on your paycheck stub. It's the rate that applies to the last dollars you earn.

Income tax applies at a low rate to the first dollars you earn and at higher rates as your income increases. As of 2015 the rates range from 10% to 39.6%. It might be more accurate to say the rates begin at 0%, because most people can claim certain deductions (the standard deduction and at least one personal exemption) that allow them to earn thousands of dollars before they pay any tax at all.

When your income reaches the level where the next rate begins to apply, each additional dollar of income is taxed at the higher rate, but the lower rates continue to apply to the money you earned earlier. For example, if your income is exactly $1,000 above the level where the 25% rate starts to apply, your tax would be $250 higher than it would be without that $1,000—but all the income you earned up to that point would continue to be taxed at rates lower than 25%. The *average* rate that applies to your income would be much lower than 25%, because almost all your income was taxed at lower rates.

> Withholding rates are designed to be roughly the same as the *average* rate of tax you pay on your income for the entire year, so your withholding rate is likely to be considerably lower than the rate that applies to the last dollars you earn.

We have to focus on the *marginal* rate (in this case 25%) instead of the much lower average rate because this is the rate that tells how much benefit you get from a deduction, and how much tax you pay on added income. If your last $1,000 of income was taxed at 25%, then you save $250 if you pick up a $1,000 deduction (such as a contribution to a traditional retirement account). Likewise, when you're taking taxable distributions, we need to know the additional tax cost of that income.

Rate shifting

Let's see what happens if your tax rate in retirement is higher than in the years you're building the account. In this situation a

Roth can produce better results than a traditional account, sometimes by a wide margin.

> **Example:** You put $2,000 into a traditional account during a year when your tax rate was 15%. Your tax benefit is $300 (15% of $2,000), so your net cost was $1,700. Many years later it has grown to ten times that amount and you withdraw $20,000—but your tax rate is now 25% and you're left with $15,000 after paying the tax. If you had put $1,700 into a Roth you would have ended up with $17,000.

The underlying reality here is something we call *rate shifting*. If you use a traditional account in this situation, you're shifting income that would have been taxed at 15% into a year when it will be taxed at 25%. At the time of the contribution the difference seems relatively small, amounting to just $200. But the difference grows as the account grows. In this example where the account grows to ten times its original value, the end result is a $2,000 reduction in spending power during retirement. A Roth account avoids this result.

Clearly you should prefer a Roth account if you expect to be in a higher tax bracket during the years you pull money out of your account. This is why Roth accounts are so attractive for young people who haven't reached the level of earnings where higher tax rates apply. The value of getting tax-exempt distributions in retirement is greater than the value of the tax benefit from contributing to a traditional account.

> A student working a summer job may not earn enough to pay any income tax at all, but the earnings can be used to support a Roth IRA contribution that may produce tax-free investment growth for several decades.

Rate shifting in the other direction

What if you're in the opposite situation? Perhaps you're in your peak earning years, paying tax at relatively high rates. You expect to be in a lower bracket during retirement. In this fairly common situation the economics of rate shifting favor a traditional account.

Before we jump to the conclusion that a traditional account will produce a better result, let's consider some reasons your tax rate in retirement may be higher than you expect.

- *Working in retirement.* More and more people work at least part time during their "retirement" years, as a way to make ends meet or for the satisfaction of doing something more productive than trying to get up and down from a greenside bunker.
- *Tax rates.* In the time since the previous edition of this book, tax rates have gone up and budget deficits have gone down. Nevertheless, the incomprehensibly huge hidden deficits in the future funding of Social Security and Medicare payments to baby boomers in retirement may lead to still higher tax rates in the future.
- *Taxable retirement benefits.* Some or all of your non-Roth retirement benefits are likely to be taxable, and the dollar amounts could be large enough to put you in a higher tax bracket than you expect.

Two special considerations that favor Roth accounts deserve special mention in connection with rate shifting: the tax treatment of Social Security benefits and the penalty tax on early withdrawals.

Social Security benefits

Social Security retirement benefits are tax-free for people with *provisional income* below certain levels: $25,000 for singles or $32,000 for couples ($0 if married filing separately). Notably, these thresholds are not indexed for inflation. Provisional income includes half your Social Security benefits and also certain items normally excluded from income, such as interest on tax-exempt bonds. More and more of the benefit becomes taxable as income rises above the specified levels until you reach the maximum, where 85% of those benefits are included in taxable income.

The income you have to take into account in determining the tax treatment of your Social Security benefit includes such items as wages, interest income, capital gains and dividends. It also includes income from retirement accounts. When you take money from a traditional IRA or 401k, you not only pay tax on that income, but also may boost the amount of Social Security income that is taxable—a double whammy.

> **Example:** Your income level might put you in the 15% tax bracket, so that normally you would pay $150 on an added $1,000 of income. But that income increases the amount of Social Security benefit that's considered taxable by $500. Although your income went up by $1,000, your *taxable* income went up by $1,500, and in the 15% tax bracket that will cost you $225. So your effective tax rate on a distribution from a traditional IRA can be 22.5%.

The rules for taxing Social Security benefits take into account some items of tax-free income, such as interest on municipal bonds. Yet tax-free withdrawals from a Roth account are *not* included. If your other income during retirement is modest, having a Roth account can help you eliminate some or all of the tax you might otherwise pay on your Social Security benefits.

Early distribution penalty

There's another way a Roth account can provide a rate shifting advantage. If you find yourself needing to pull money out of a retirement account before age 59½, you may have to pay a 10% penalty. This penalty applies only to the taxable part of the distribution, however. (There's an exception for conversion dollars withdrawn within five years after the conversion.) In a traditional account, the entire distribution is usually taxable, so the penalty applies to the full amount. With a Roth account, even when you take a nonqualifying distribution, you can usually treat some or all of it as nontaxable, reducing or eliminating this penalty.

The rules for distributions depend on which type of Roth account you have. A Roth IRA allows you to withdraw your contributions before you withdraw any investment earnings. It's like having a "Get out of IRA Free" card: you pay no tax or penalty on those distributions. If you take a nonqualifying distribution from a Roth account in an employer plan, the tax rules divide that distribution proportionately between a return of your contributions and a payout of the account's earnings. The part treated as earnings will be taxable and potentially subject to the 10% penalty, but you're still better off than if you paid tax and penalty on the entire amount.

> This isn't all good. Your ability to tap this money at no immediate cost could lead you to overlook the long-term cost of reducing your tax-free retirement savings. If you succumb to temptation, you'll have less wealth in retirement. That's the most important "penalty" of an early withdrawal.

The availability of penalty-free withdrawals can help in another way. If you want to keep some of your money available to cover emergencies, it wouldn't make sense to put that money in a traditional IRA. The 10% penalty would hit at just the wrong time. You don't have that concern with a Roth IRA, though, so you can be more aggressive in funding the account.

> **Example:** You're trying to decide how much money to stuff into your IRA. You have $2,500 available for this purpose, but you're concerned that you might need some of that money for a car repair or other emergency. If you're saving in a traditional IRA, you might be smarter to keep some of that money outside the IRA, so you won't have to pay a penalty if that need arises. But you can put the entire amount into a Roth, knowing that in an emergency you can take some of that money out without paying any tax or penalty.

Once you get that extra money into your IRA, you should be disciplined, even tenacious, in trying to keep it there. Yet knowing you have penalty-free access can help you get it there in the first place. This is a significant benefit that never appears in the calculations used to choose between traditional and Roth accounts.

Choosing a traditional account

If you take all these factors into account and still believe your tax rate is likely to be lower when you pull money out of your account, it's possible that a traditional account will be a better choice for you. A Roth account will produce tax-free investment earnings, but a traditional account can produce an even better result by shifting earnings into a year when lower tax rates apply.

Yet the other benefits of Roth accounts can overcome a rate-shifting advantage, especially if you maintain the account for a long enough time. If you'll pay 33% on a conversion, for example, but expect a 25% tax rate during retirement, you can still come out ahead with the conversion if you keep the account for another fifteen years or so. The time needed for the Roth to pull ahead depends on guesses about investment returns during the relevant period, but it's within the range of a reasonable investment horizon.

When a traditional account wins. If we assume you'll preserve the benefit of the tax deduction, a Roth's advantages will rarely overcome that big 10-point gap between the 15% rate and the 25% rate. Generally it won't make sense to pay 25% or more on a conversion if you expect to pay no more than 15% on money you would withdraw from a traditional account during retirement. Keep in mind the tax savings preservation fallacy, though (Chapter 4), especially if you're choosing an account for annual saving rather than thinking about a Roth conversion.

> As of 2015, it takes roughly $50,000 of gross income to push a single taxpayer over 65 into the 25% bracket, assuming no deductions other than the standard deduction and a personal exemption (double that on a joint return).

9

IRA vs. Employer Account

Where to stash your retirement savings when you're eligible for a 401k or similar account.

IF YOU'RE ELIGIBLE TO PARTICIPATE in an employer's 401k or 403b plan you have a choice of where to save: in the employer plan, in an IRA, or both. Your choice may be influenced by several factors discussed below:

- Matching contributions
- Investments
- Expenses
- Account access

We'll turn to those issues after a brief discussion of how participation in an employer plan affects your IRA contributions.

Eligibility

Your employer should let you know if you're eligible to participate in a 401k or 403b plan. Assuming you're eligible, you may wonder how participation in that plan will affect your contributions to an IRA.

Contrary to popular belief, contributing to an employer plan does not reduce your eligibility to contribute to an IRA. In the case of a Roth IRA, you may actually qualify for a *larger* contribution when you also put money in a 401k or similar plan. That's because contributing to one of these plans can reduce your taxable income (if the money goes to a traditional account), and Roth IRA contribution limits are phased out at higher income levels.

In the case of traditional IRAs, your participation in an employer plan does not affect the amount you can contribute, but it may affect the amount you can *deduct*. Determining whether you're a "participant" in a 401k or 403b plan for purposes of this rule can be tricky, and doesn't necessarily depend on whether you made a contribution that year. A checkbox in box 13 of Form W-2 labeled "retirement plan" indicates this status.

A phase-out rule for the deduction applies when your income rises above specified levels if you participate in an employer plan (or, at different income levels, if your spouse does). In this situation you're still allowed to put money in a traditional IRA, but your contributions will be nondeductible. Naturally you would do better putting your money in a Roth IRA when your contributions are nondeductible, but if you can't contribute to a Roth because your income is too high or because you're married filing separately, you still have the option of making a nondeductible contribution to a traditional IRA.

> If you find yourself in this situation, you may want to consider the *backdoor Roth IRA contribution* technique discussed in Chapter 16.

Matching contributions

Many employers that offer 401k or similar plans will provide a partial match of contributions up to a specified limit. For example, an employer might add 25 cents to your account for each of the first $6,000 you contribute. Matching contributions may come with a vesting requirement, meaning you can lose them (and any earnings they generate) if you don't remain employed with the company long enough.

If you stick around long enough for this part of your account to become vested, the result is a handsome boost in your retirement savings. If you start out with $125 for every $100 you add to the account, that's like getting three or more extra years of solid investment earnings—without the need to pick good investments or take investment risk. It's tough to beat that kind of benefit, even if you're comparing a traditional account with the advantages of a Roth IRA. Most experts say your first priority for retirement savings is to qualify for the maximum matching contribution, and I have to agree.

Investments

Investment performance is one of the biggest factors in determining how much wealth you'll have in retirement. The investments available for an employer plan account are usually chosen by a retirement plan committee. If those choices are not very good, you may prefer saving in an IRA. Depending on where you establish your IRA, you can invest it in just about anything that would be allowed in an employer account.

One exception: many employer plans offer *stable value funds*, which are generally not available outside of employer plans. Also, retirement plans may qualify for an "institutional" class of mutual fund shares with lower fees (and therefore better performance) than shares sold to the general public. These relatively minor advantages are worth noting but may be outweighed by other factors.

Fortunately, most employers make it a high priority to offer excellent investments for their retirement plan accounts. At some companies you can invest your account just about any way you might imagine. Others offer a limited selection of well-chosen mutual funds—and that may be even better than a bewildering array that gives you more chances to go wrong. If you run into a truly unsatisfactory menu of choices, though, you may want to hesitate before committing money to your employer's plan.

Expenses

Another key factor determining how your retirement account will perform is the level of expenses it has to bear. Some of the expenses, such as management fees charged by mutual funds, are associated with particular investments. An employer plan will also incur administrative expenses, which your company may or may not charge against individual accounts.

This is a key issue, but historically it has been difficult to find the information you need. Rules that made it easier for plan participants to learn about expenses their accounts bear took effect in 2012. Pay attention when you receive this information from your employer, because it's important.

An IRA can hold excellent investments and have annual fees, including mutual fund fees, less than 0.5% per year. (That's true of my personal IRA, and I didn't get any special deals). It's normal for 401k participants to pay at least double that amount, which may be reasonable, all things considered. If you see a number that's pushing toward 2% per year or more, you have a right to be grumpy, and perhaps a reason to save in an IRA instead of that plan, as expenses that high eat away too much of the investment earnings.

> See Chapter 27 for more on investing your retirement account.

Account access

It may be useful to understand differences in your ability to get your hands on the money in your account. Some of these differences favor IRAs and others favor employer plans.

- Subject to limitations, many employers allow 401k or 403b plan participants to borrow from their accounts. These loans aren't necessarily a good idea, but if you need the money, it's good to have this option available. You aren't allowed to borrow from an IRA.
- Although some plans permit in-service withdrawals, the general rule for 401k and similar plans is that you can't withdraw your money while still working for the employer. Most plans allow "hardship" withdrawals if you meet certain requirements, but otherwise you may not be able to gain access to the money, even though it's fully vested and represents your own contributions.
- You can demand a withdrawal from an IRA whenever you want, provided you haven't tied it up in an illiquid investment. The taxable portion of a withdrawal taken before age 59½ is subject to a 10% penalty unless you qualify for an exception. Here again, this may not be your best financial move but you can get your hands on the money if you really need it.

The usual order of preference

Individual factors may lead you to make a choice different from the one that's best for most people, but the usual order of preference for retirement savings would be as follows. If the first choice isn't available, or you've saved up to the relevant limit for that choice, move on to the next one. This list assumes you have an overall preference for a Roth account.

- If your employer offers a Roth 401k or similar plan with matching contributions, make your first contributions there, at least to the limit of the matching contributions.
- If your employer offers only a traditional 401k or 403b, but offers matching contributions, you have to choose between the benefits of a Roth account and the benefit of the match. It's usually best to choose the match unless you expect to leave that job before the matching money becomes vested.

> If you're in this situation, you should be asking the employer to consider adding Roth accounts to the 401k or 403b plan. The benefits of these accounts to the participants far outweigh the costs to the employer. Yet some employers figure there's no point in offering the benefit unless workers show an interest, so speak up! Your interest in this benefit will help the company justify the costs of adding Roth accounts to the plan.

- When you've soaked up all the matching contributions that are available, get your next dollars into a Roth account. If you have a choice between Roth IRA and Roth account with your employer at this point, you may want to favor the Roth IRA. That's because you already stuffed money into the employer account to absorb the match, and you'll have more flexibility if you split your savings between different types of accounts.

- When you've reached the limit of what you can put in Roth accounts, additional dollars would go into traditional accounts to the extent pre-tax contributions are still available. For example, if your employer offers only a traditional 401k, you would contribute there up to the limit of the matching contribution, then to your Roth IRA up to that limit, and then put additional dollars in the 401k.

You may find yourself in a position where the only retirement account contribution allowed is a nondeductible contribution to a traditional IRA. It's questionable whether these contributions make sense at today's tax rates. These accounts provide deferral of the tax on investment earnings, but those earnings end up being taxed as ordinary income. You might do just as well or better with savings in a regular investment account if your investment style allows you to be tax-efficient.

> You shouldn't feel that the limits imposed on retirement accounts prevent you from saving even more. If you invest in a tax-efficient manner, savings placed in a regular account can perform nearly as well as formal retirement accounts.

10

The Conversion Decision

The decision whether to convert to a Roth IRA is similar to the decision whether to contribute to a Roth account in the first place—but with a few notable differences.

THE PRECEDING CHAPTERS DISCUSS REASONS to put your retirement savings into a Roth account. If you've already accumulated savings in a traditional account, you may want to consider converting that account to a Roth IRA if you're eligible to do so. Conversion can produce huge benefits in the long run, for many of the reasons we've already discussed. There are some additional points that are unique to conversions.

See also Chapters 24 and 25. The availability of conversion strategies, especially the advanced strategies discussed in Chapter 25, may affect the desirability of a conversion.

Expanding your account

We saw in Chapter 6 that a Roth account can have a greater effective size than a traditional account because qualifying Roth distributions are not taxable. The increase in effective size depends on the tax rate that would apply to distributions from a traditional account. You can achieve the same increase by converting a traditional account to a Roth IRA, provided that you don't use money from the retirement account to pay tax on the conversion.

> **Example:** You have a $40,000 traditional account. You're in the 25% bracket and expect to be in that bracket during the years you take distributions. The 25% tax means the effective value of this account is $30,000. If you convert it to a Roth IRA, paying the $10,000 conversion tax from other resources, you'll have a Roth IRA that is permanently tax-free with an effective value of $40,000.

This ability to expand the effective size of your retirement account is such an important benefit that some people say you shouldn't convert to a Roth IRA if you'll have to use part of the account to pay the conversion tax. Yet conversion can produce other benefits even if you have to pay some or all of the tax from the account.

Drawing money from your retirement account to pay tax on a conversion could expose you to 10% the early withdrawal penalty. The benefits of conversion are rarely great enough to overcome the detriment of paying a 10% early distribution penalty, but that concern falls away when you reach age 59½. At that point you can consider a Roth conversion even if you have to use part of the account to pay the conversion tax, for reasons discussed below.

Avoiding minimum distributions

As we saw in Chapter 7, Roth IRAs can provide a significant advantage because the minimum distribution rules don't apply during the lifetime of the original owner. If you're one of those people who prefer not to have this annual requirement to withdraw part of your retirement savings beginning at age 70½, conversion to a Roth IRA may make sense.

Taxation of Social Security benefits

We also noted earlier that a Roth can provide a benefit because of the way Social Security benefits are taxed. You have to pay tax on up to 85% of these benefits, but the amount you report as income depends on your overall level of income. Unless your income is already high enough so you pay tax on the maximum amount, a Roth conversion can reduce the amount of tax you pay on those benefits.

> Note that a Roth conversion can *increase* the tax on your Social Security benefits in the year of conversion, if you're already receiving benefits at the time of the conversion. Potential savings come in years after the conversion.

Medicare premiums

At certain levels, additional income can lead to an increase in Medicare premiums. A Roth conversion can eliminate the need to report income from annual retirement account distributions that may affect your Medicare premiums year after year. Be aware, though, that the Roth conversion income can put you into a higher income category for one year, and the resulting one-year change in Medicare premiums can be an added cost of doing a conversion if you're at or near the age to be enrolled in that program.

> There's a time lag in this income effect. When the government determines your Medicare premium for a given year, they don't know what your income for that year will be, or even what your income for the *preceding* year was, because you may not file that return until April 15, or even later if you file on extension. Typically they're looking two years back because that's the most recent year for which data is available. That means income from a conversion in 2015 could increase your Medicare premium for 2017—and possibly reduce it for years after 2017.

Rate shifting

We saw in Chapter 8 that rate shifting can work for or against you when you choose a Roth account. The same is true in a Roth conversion, but with a special concern. If the account is large enough, the dollar amount of the conversion may push you into a higher tax bracket than usual. This is an unfavorable condition for conversion.

> **Example:** You're normally in the 15% tax bracket and expect to be in that bracket during retirement. Converting your $40,000 traditional IRA to a Roth will push you into the 25% bracket, however. Half the conversion income will be taxed at 15% but the other half will be taxed at 25%.

In this situation you may want to consider converting half the account in one year and the other half a year later. This approach is perfectly acceptable, and keeps all the income in the 15% bracket.

> There is one potential drawback when you convert an account over a period of years. If your investments rise in value before you complete the conversion, you'll pay tax on a greater amount of income, even though you benefit from paying tax at a lower rate.

Occasionally we hear from someone who has an unusual opportunity to convert to a Roth IRA at a lower than normal rate. It might be someone who took a year off from work, or someone who has unusually high deductions, and as a result will pay far less tax than normal on the conversion income. If you have an opportunity like this, by all means, seize it!

A hidden benefit

Now let me tell you about a great hidden benefit in converting to a Roth IRA. This benefit can save you thousands of dollars in the right circumstances. It arises from the recharacterization rules, which let you undo a conversion until October 15 of the year after the conversion. These rules are intended mainly to correct mistakes, but you can also use them to undo a conversion simply because it didn't turn out to be favorable.

The benefit here is mainly for people who have a significant part of their account invested in stocks. As you probably know, stocks have historically provided very strong investment performance over the long run, but in the short run they can do just about anything, including a steep drop. Let's use an example to see how you can use the recharacterization rules to your advantage.

Example: In January you convert an IRA worth $100,000. That means you have to report $100,000 of income on the return you'll file in April of the following year. Fair enough. But now let's take another look at the situation

> in October, twenty-one months after the conversion. One possibility is the stock market roared ahead, and the account is now worth $140,000. That's great! You avoided paying tax on $40,000 of growth!
>
> But there's another possibility. Suppose the stock market went south, leaving you with an account worth $70,000. That's bad news, and it seems even worse when you consider that you paid tax on $100,000. No problem: you can undo the conversion, and recover the entire tax as if it never happened. Then you wait a while (there's a required waiting period) and convert again at the lower value. Result: you avoid paying tax on that $30,000 in stock market losses.

These rules work almost like having a stock option. You gain a benefit if the stock market goes up after the conversion, but avoid a detriment if the stock market goes down. This is why I tell people who are sitting on the fence to go ahead with a conversion. For any given year, the deadline for doing a conversion is December 31, but the deadline for *undoing* a conversion doesn't come until October 15 of the following year. See Chapter 23 for details.

Converting in retirement

Some people think of a Roth conversion as something that can pay off only if you expect to leave the account untouched for many years. They assume it doesn't make sense to do a Roth conversion if you're already retired, or even if you're close to retirement. Yet you can gain significant benefits from converting to a Roth late in life.

Some of the reasons were mentioned earlier in this chapter. For example, if you can pay the conversion tax from other sources, you'll have increased the effective size of your retirement account. Dipping into the account to pay the conversion tax isn't necessarily as bad as it would be for a younger person, though, because the 10% early withdrawal penalty doesn't apply to people over age 59½. That's true even if you're taking money from the Roth within five years after the conversion.

Likewise, you may be in a position now to clearly see how a conversion will affect taxation of your Social Security benefits. If you're already receiving those benefits, the income you report as a result of the conversion may cause you to pay more tax on those benefits in the year of the conversion. In subsequent years, though, you can take money from your Roth IRA without increasing the taxable part of your social security benefits. See also the earlier discussion of Medicare premiums.

Conversion can also make sense if you expect to leave the account to your beneficiaries. Perhaps you can convert at a tax rate that's lower than your beneficiaries would pay if you left them a traditional IRA. Conversion can also produce estate tax savings. Retirement accounts are included in your estate, whether they are Roth or conventional accounts. But the tax you pay at the time of the conversion reduces the size of your estate, so it may reduce the amount of estate tax.

11

Saving for Other Goals

Although Roth accounts are designed for retirement savings, the tax rules for Roth IRAs make them suitable for other types of savings.

RETIREMENT IS ONLY ONE OF THE MAJOR GOALS for which people save. You may be saving for the purchase of a home, or for your children's college education, or for other purposes. Normally you would not want to use a traditional IRA for such savings because of the tax hit when you pull the money out—often accompanied by a 10% early distribution penalty tax. A Roth IRA may make sense for such savings, though.

The main reason to consider a Roth IRA is a rule that allows you to withdraw your regular contributions at any time, free of tax or penalty. As explained in Part VI, you may have to pay tax or an early distribution penalty (or both) if you don't wait long enough before withdrawing investment earnings or conversion money. But contributions come out before any other amounts. A special rule can make the Roth even better if you're saving to buy a home.

General savings

Most of us want to have at least some savings that aren't dedicated to retirement. You may want to set aside money as an emergency fund, or to cover a dream vacation, or for any other major expenditure that may occur before you retire. You can keep that money in a regular investment account with a bank, mutual fund or brokerage company. You'll pay tax on the investment earnings as you go along, and you may have to report a capital gain when you sell assets to withdraw the money, but you won't have to deal with any special tax rules when you use the money.

Why use a Roth IRA? If you aren't already maximizing your contributions to a Roth IRA, you can put general savings in the account along with the money you plan to use for retirement. When you need to tap the general savings, you can pull money out free of tax or penalty as long as the total amount you withdraw is no greater than the total amount you contributed.

> **Example:** You want to put away $2,000 a year toward your retirement, and at the same time you're saving $2,000 toward another personal goal for which you'll need $10,000.

One approach is to put $2,000 per year in a Roth IRA and another $2,000 per year in a regular savings account. If you do that, you'll pay tax on any investment earnings on the money you keep outside the IRA. Instead, you can put the entire $4,000 per year in the Roth IRA (assuming you qualify to contribute that amount). Eventually you can withdraw the $10,000 you need for another purpose, without paying tax or penalty, provided that the total amount you withdraw is no more than the total amount contributed. Investment earnings will remain in the account and will eventually qualify for tax-free withdrawal.

> The end result is to avoid paying tax on interest or other investment earnings generated by money you're saving for another purpose.

If you wish, you can use your own personal accounting to determine when you've reached the amount needed for your alternative goal. In the example above, you might find that the account has grown to $20,000 at a time when your total contributions are $16,000. You've contributed $8,000 for retirement and $8,000 for your other goal, and the account includes $4,000 of investment earnings, half of which relate to the money saved for the other goal. You might choose to "declare victory" for your other goal, take the $10,000 out of the account and spend it as you planned. From your perspective, you're using $2,000 of the account's earnings for this goal, but as far as the IRS is concerned the $10,000 withdrawal comes from the $16,000 in contributions. You're left with an account that holds $6,000 in contributions and $4,000 in earnings.

Saving for college

Special considerations apply if you're saving for college. There are other types of accounts designed for this purpose: 529 accounts and Coverdell accounts. These accounts work much like Roth IRAs, allowing you to make nondeductible contributions, build up investment earnings inside the account, and eventually withdraw the money, including earnings, without paying any tax if the money is used for college expenses.

As we just saw, you can achieve the same results using a Roth IRA, provided that two things are true:

- The total amount you're saving for retirement and college is within the limit of what you're allowed to save in a Roth IRA, and
- The total amount you'll withdraw before meeting the requirements for qualifying Roth IRA distributions is no more than the total amount of your contributions (in other words, you won't dip into the account's earnings to pay for college expenses).

When those conditions don't exist, you're likely to be better off using a 529 or Coverdell account for college savings. You'll be hurting yourself on the front end (not saving enough because of the limit) or on the back end (paying tax on earnings withdrawn before retirement). If your situation happens to fit those two requirements, though, a Roth IRA can be a good place for college savings. In some situations it may work out better than if you used a 529 or Coverdell account.

The biggest advantage for the Roth IRA comes if you don't end up using the money for college. Your child may end up not going to college, or may earn a scholarship that eliminates the need to tap your savings. In this event you'll lose at least some of the tax benefits of saving in a 529 or Coverdell account. If you put this money into a Roth IRA, you can simply leave it there as part of your retirement savings.

> Meanwhile, if you do use money from your Roth IRA for your child's college expenses, you can still leave investment earnings in the account to be withdrawn tax-free at a later time.

Another possibility: an emergency of some sort requires you to tap money that was set aside for college. You may feel that this money is sacred and should never be used for any other purpose. Life holds surprises, though, and you could find yourself in a situation where pulling money from the college savings account is the lesser of two evils. In this situation, the rule allowing tax-free withdrawals of contributions from a Roth IRA can ease the pain. With a 529 or Coverdell account, you have to treat part of your withdrawal as taxable investment earnings, even before you've taken out all your contributions.

There are a number of other considerations, some favoring the Roth IRA and some favoring 529 or Coverdell accounts. Depending on where you live, you may receive a state income tax benefit when you contribute to the state's 529 plan. Yet the investment opportunities in your state's 529 plan may not be as good as those you can find for your Roth IRA. Using a 529 or Coverdell account will allow you to use the account's investment earnings tax-free for college expenses. To avoid paying tax on the Roth IRA's investment earnings you'll have to leave them in the account until you meet the requirements described in Part VI.

> Money in a Roth IRA doesn't count as parental assets under the federal formula for student financial aid, but some schools use a different formula that may count this money. What's more, withdrawals from a Roth IRA may count as income in the formula even though they don't count as income on your tax return.

Saving for a home

There's a special rule that allows you to take a tax-free distribution of earnings from a Roth IRA for the purpose of buying a home. To qualify, you have to be a *first-time homebuyer*, which strangely enough is not necessarily someone who has never before owned a home. You also need to have a Roth IRA at least five years before you take money out for this purpose. See Chapter 31 for details on this rule.

Remember, you don't have to use this rule if the total amount you withdraw from your Roth IRA is less than the total amount of your contributions. This rule comes into play only if you withdraw some or all of the investment earnings.

Part III
Contributions to Roth Accounts

12 How to Start a Roth IRA

13 Roth IRA Contributions

14 Qualifying Income for IRA Contributions

15 Income Limitation for Roth IRA Contributions

16 Backdoor Roth IRA Contributions

17 Roth Accounts in 401k and Similar Plans

18 Retirement Savings Contributions Credit

19 Retroactive Switching

20 Troubleshooting Contributions

12

How to Start a Roth IRA

Practical guidance on how to set up a Roth IRA.

STARTING A ROTH 401K OR SIMILAR ACCOUNT usually involves filling out some forms provided by your employer. If you have any questions, you can get answers from the nice folks in the human resources department. Starting a Roth IRA requires a little more effort on your part. This chapter walks you through the process.

Outline

To start a Roth IRA you need to take the following steps:

- Determine that a Roth IRA is your best choice.
- Confirm that you're eligible for a Roth IRA.
- Decide what type of investment is most appropriate for your Roth IRA.

- Select a provider for your Roth IRA.
- Establish the IRA.

Choosing the Roth IRA

Naturally, before you set up a Roth IRA you want to determine whether a Roth IRA is the right choice for your retirement savings. If you're unsure at this point, turn back to Part II of this book, where we discuss the issue in some detail.

Eligibility

It's your responsibility, not the IRA provider's, to determine that you're eligible to establish a Roth IRA. And there's no point in setting one up if you'll merely have to undo the process later. Eligibility rules are summarized in Chapter 2 and covered in more detail in the chapters following this one.

Eligibility for a contribution depends in part on your "modified adjusted gross income." Some people don't get a good handle on this number until their tax return is prepared. By that time you've missed a chance for any investment earnings that would have built up in the account if you made your contributions earlier. Fortunately there are ways to correct any problems that occur if you make a contribution that isn't allowed. So make your best estimate based on the available information and, if it appears you're eligible, move ahead with your plan.

> To estimate your adjusted gross income for a year that's not yet completed, it's usually best to begin with your adjusted gross income from the preceding year's tax return and estimate any changes from there.

Type of investment

The next step is to figure out what kind of investments you plan to make. Chapter 27 provides guidance in this area, but here are some preliminary thoughts.

Size of your Roth IRA. The tax law doesn't set a minimum size for a Roth IRA, but many providers set minimum account sizes. If one provider won't accept your account because it's too small, try another. In any event, if you're starting small, it makes sense to choose a simple investment that won't incur a lot of fees or require a lot of attention. You can get fancy after you've built your IRA to a larger size.

> Many providers will allow you to start an IRA with an initial amount that's smaller than their usual minimum if you sign up for automatic monthly contributions.

Time frame. When investing for the long term (which is typical for retirement savings) it makes sense to take some risk to obtain higher rewards. If the risk produces losses, you'll have plenty of time to recover. Short term investors need to put more emphasis on asset protection.

Your other investments. If you have other savings, such as a brokerage account or a 401k account, consider whether your IRA can be invested in a way that provides more balance to your overall portfolio. Another consideration is the allocation of assets between taxable accounts and non-taxable accounts. For example, some advisors suggest keeping assets that produce mostly ordinary income (like interest or dividends that don't qualify for the 15% rate) in an IRA or other non-taxable account, and investing taxable accounts in assets that produce long-term capital gain or qualifying dividends. See Chapter 27 for discussion.

Your investing style. Choose an investment you're comfortable with. Some investors are willing to risk losses in order to have a shot at higher gains. Others are willing to accept a lower return to get a greater feeling of security.

Investing style affects your choice in another way. Some types of investments do quite well if you ignore them for extended periods. Others need frequent attention. How much time and effort do you want to put into your IRA investments?

Select a provider

It's easy enough to find an IRA provider. But which one is best for you?

Banks. For this purpose, "banks" include trust companies, savings and loans, and credit unions as well as commercial banks. Banks often accept relatively small accounts (some have no minimum at all) and have simple procedures, making them an attractive choice for people who want to start out small. But they'll gladly accept larger accounts! A bank isn't likely to offer as many investment alternatives as a mutual fund company or brokerage firm.

Mutual funds. Mutual fund companies offer a wide range of investments. You may be able to invest parts of your IRA in different types of funds, or you may find a single fund that provides the mix that's right for you. Some mutual fund companies make it easy to shift some or all of your IRA from one fund to another when your investment objectives change.

Brokerage firms. You can also start a Roth IRA as a brokerage account. These accounts give you the ability to invest in individual stocks or bonds. Some brokerage firms allow you to mix mutual funds and stock holdings in the same account.

Insurance companies. Insurance companies provide IRAs, too. This choice may be appealing if you want to invest in an annuity or you find some other investment offering of the insurance company attractive.

> Annuity investments in IRAs are controversial. Before making this investment, get an opinion from an unbiased source: someone who won't earn a commission when you make the investment.

Fees. Before you settle on a particular provider, ask about the fees that will apply to your account. There may be startup fees, annual maintenance fees, fees for changing your investments or withdrawing your money. These fees can have a significant impact on the investment performance of your IRA. It's especially important to find out ahead of time what would be involved if you decide you want to transfer your account to another provider.

> For a while, one prominent tax return preparation company encouraged its customers to put tax refunds into IRAs with expenses so high that in many cases it was impossible to earn a positive investment return.

IRAs for minors. There's no minimum age to start an IRA, provided the child has qualifying income as described in Chapter 14. Yet there are other legal issues that initially made it hard to find a custodian that would accept an IRA account for a minor. Many of the major financial firms now offer these accounts, so you shouldn't have too much difficulty finding a provider if you want to establish an IRA for a minor.

Establish your IRA

Establishing your IRA can be as simple as walking into a bank or brokerage office, filling out a few forms (make sure you have your social security number!) and writing a check. You can also set up an IRA over the Internet if the provider you prefer does business that way. There are a few points to keep in mind when you establish your account.

Beneficiaries. You're permitted to determine who receives your IRA at your death. Chances are the form presented to you by the IRA provider will say it goes to your spouse, if you have a living spouse at your death, and otherwise goes to your estate. This isn't necessarily the best choice. You can change the beneficiary later, but most people forget about this, so it's a good idea to get it right when you establish the account. Don't forget you can name a contingent beneficiary in case the first beneficiary dies before you do.

> If you're putting a substantial amount into your IRA, it may make sense to consult an estate planning professional about the beneficiary designation.

Record keeping

Finally there's the little matter of record keeping. Make sure you have a safe place for all records pertaining to your IRA, where you'll be able to get at them when it's time to fill out your income tax return or make a change in your investments. You aren't required to report regular contributions to a Roth IRA, however, unless you also took distributions from your Roth IRA.

13

Roth IRA Contributions

Most people who work for a living, and many who do not, can contribute to a Roth IRA.

HERE'S A CHECKLIST FOR DETERMINING whether you can contribute to a Roth IRA for a particular year:

- The total of all your contributions to IRAs for the year (traditional and Roth) must be within an overall limit described below.
- You (or your spouse, if you file jointly) need to have *qualifying income* at least equal to the amount of your contributions. Details of this requirement appear in Chapter 14.
- If your income is above a level specified for your filing status, your contribution limit is reduced, possibly all the way to zero. Details of this requirement appear in Chapter 15.

That's it! If you meet these requirements you can contribute, no matter how young or old you may be, and even if you also contribute to a 401k or similar plan.

The overall limit

The overall limit for IRAs is the maximum amount you can contribute, assuming you have enough qualifying income. It's a single limit that applies to the total amount you contribute to traditional IRAs and Roth IRAs. You're allowed to contribute to both types of IRA in the same year, but you have to keep the total within this limit.

As of 2015, people under 50 can contribute $5,500 per year. This figure will be adjusted for inflation in later years.

> The limit changes only when the inflation adjustment is big enough to reach a $500 increment. Due to low inflation, it has remained at $5,500 since 2013.

If you're age 50 or older by the end of the year, you can contribute another $1,000 for that year. This $1,000 increment is not adjusted for inflation, but continues to be tacked on when the base number changes. For example, when the limit for people under 50 goes to $5,500, the limit for people 50 and older will be $6,500.

> To qualify for the additional $1,000 you have to reach age 50 by the end of the year for which you are contributing. For purposes of this rule, if your birthday is January 1, the IRS treats you as being age 50 on December 31 of the previous year.

Reduction for other contributions

The amount you can contribute to a Roth IRA is reduced for certain other contributions:

- Contributions you make to a traditional IRA (other than rollover contributions).
- Contributions you make to a "501(c)(18) plan." These are pension plans created before June 25, 1959 that are funded entirely with employee contributions.

Your Roth IRA contribution is not reduced or otherwise affected by any contribution you make to a 401k or similar plan.

Q: What if I contribute to a SEP IRA or SIMPLE IRA?

A: Typically these contributions are salary reduction contributions, similar to 401k contributions. These do not reduce the contribution you can make to a Roth IRA.

Q: But there's an exception?

A: Yes. You're permitted to make a regular "IRA-type" contribution to a SEP IRA (subject to the same dollar limit that applies to any other IRA contribution). If you make this type of contribution to a SEP IRA, in addition to any "employer-type" contribution you make to your SEP IRA, it reduces the amount you can contribute to a Roth IRA.

When to contribute

You can make your contribution for a given tax year any time from the first day of that year until the due date, without extensions, for that year's tax return. For most people that means April 15 of the following year. If the tax return due date is delayed because it falls on a weekend or holiday, the later deadline applies to IRA contributions as well. You don't have to make the contribution before you file the return, but the money has to go into the account by the *due date* of the return.

> **Mailing rule doesn't apply.** If your tax return is due April 15, you can meet the filing deadline by mailing your return that day. This rule doesn't apply to IRA contributions. You have to get the money into your account by the deadline, and that means sending it to the trustee far enough ahead of time so the check is received and processed by April 15.

Overlap period. Contributions made between January 1 and the due date of your return can be for the current year or the previous year. This overlap has resulted in countless errors as contributions were recorded for the wrong year. Mistakes can be costly, causing you to lose the opportunity to contribute for one year and incur a penalty for contributions over the limit in another. Be sure to indicate the correct year when you make your contribution, and follow up to confirm that the IRA provider followed your instructions.

Questions and answers about contributions

Here are some questions people ask about contributions to a Roth IRA.

Q: Is there a maximum age for contributions?

A: No! For traditional IRAs, you lose the ability to make contributions in the year you turn age 70½. Not so for Roth IRAs. If you meet the other requirements, you can set up a brand new Roth IRA at age 85 and begin saving for your "retirement"! Remember, though, you need to have qualifying income, or be married to someone who has qualifying income.

Q: Is there a minimum age for contributions?

A: No! In theory a two-year-old can have a Roth IRA. Once again, the practical concern may be the requirement to have qualifying income, which is discussed in Chapter 14.

Q: What if I participate in an employer plan?

A: Coverage under a retirement plan maintained by your employer does not affect your ability to contribute to a Roth IRA. You can contribute to a Roth IRA in the same year you contribute to a 401k or similar account, or otherwise participate in an employer's retirement plan.

Q: Can I contribute to a traditional IRA in the same year?

A: Yes, but the overall limit described earlier applies to total contributions to IRAs. If you contribute the maximum amount to a traditional IRA, you can't contribute to a Roth for the same year.

Q: Can I contribute to more than one Roth IRA in the same year?

A: Yes, but once again, the overall limit applies to the total amount you contribute to *all* your IRAs.

Q: What about making contributions in the same year I did a conversion?

A: No problem. You can contribute to a Roth IRA the same year you convert a traditional retirement account to a Roth. Better still, the income you report as a result of the conversion doesn't count in determining your contribution limit.

Q: Can I contribute to a conversion Roth IRA?

A: For a short while after Congress created the Roth IRA there was confusion about whether people would be allowed to make regular contributions to a Roth IRA that was created by converting a traditional IRA. But it's been clear for a long time now that you can combine conversion money and regular contributions in a single Roth IRA.

Q: Can I contribute if I'm married filing separately?

A: Strictly speaking, the rules allow you to contribute to a Roth IRA for a year you're married filing separately. We'll see in Chapter 15, though, that the income limit is so low that most people in this category will not be able to make Roth IRA contributions.

Q: Can I have a joint IRA with my spouse?

A: Sorry, no can do. The "I" in IRA stands for "individual." Your spouse can be the death beneficiary but can't be co-owner while you're alive. If you commingle your IRA with any other funds, including your spouse's IRA, you disqualify it.

Q: I have some stock that's gone up in value. Can I transfer that stock into my IRA as a contribution?

A: No, all contributions have to be in cash. You can move assets other than cash into an IRA only when doing a rollover, conversion or recharacterization.

Q: Will I be treated as making a contribution if I cover my IRA's investment expenses?

A: See the discussion in Chapter 26.

Repayment contributions

As a general rule, you can't return money to an IRA after you withdraw it. Unless you're returning the money within 60 days under the rollover rules, or taking advantage of a special rule for first-time homebuyers, you're stuck with the usual rules that govern IRA contributions. But Congress has created special repayment rules for *qualified reservist distributions*. If you were a reservist or national guardsman called to active duty after September 11, 2001 for a period of more than 179 days or for an indefinite period, and want to repay money you took from a retirement plan after being called to duty, check the rules in IRS Publication 3, which can be viewed or downloaded free of charge at www.irs.gov.

Congress has also passed laws allowing repayment contributions following specified natural disasters, but as of this writing the time limits for using these special rules has expired.

Military death benefits

The Heroes Earnings Assistance and Relief Tax Act of 2008 includes a provision allowing the recipient of a military death gratuity or SGLI payment to contribute that amount to a Roth

IRA. (Some or all of these amounts may instead be contributed to a Coverdell education savings account.) This contribution is treated as a rollover, except it doesn't count for purposes of the rule limiting you to a single rollover within a one-year period. As a result, it isn't subject to the annual contribution limit or the income limitation. You receive basis for this contribution, so you don't have to pay tax or the 10% early distribution penalty when you withdraw the money, even in a nonqualifying distribution. It appears, however, that you may be required to withdraw money from an earlier conversion before withdrawing this money, and that withdrawal could result in an early distribution penalty if you're under 59½ years of age and the conversion occurred within the five years preceding the withdrawal. Any earnings produced by these contributions would be subject to the usual rules.

As to deaths from injuries occurring on or after June 17, 2008, this special contribution to a Roth IRA must be made within a year after the death benefit is received. Contributions relating to deaths from injuries occurring before that date, but on or after October 7, 2001, were permitted until June 17, 2009.

14

Qualifying Income for IRA Contributions

IRA contributions have to be supported by qualifying income.

FOR EACH YEAR YOU CONTRIBUTE to an IRA, you (or your spouse, if you file jointly) must have qualifying income at least equal to the amount of the contribution. The rules described in this chapter apply to traditional IRAs as well as Roth IRAs. Some of the questions in this area are more important for Roth IRAs, however.

Qualifying income

Qualifying income is income that falls into one of these categories, which are explained below:

- Amounts earned as an employee

- Net earnings from self-employment
- Alimony income

You can't rely on other kinds of income, such as dividends and interest, to support your IRA contribution. Furthermore, the income used to support an IRA contribution generally has to be *taxable* income. There's an exception for nontaxable combat pay.

> Without qualifying income you can't contribute, even if you have other types of income.

Amounts earned as an employee

If you work as an employee, qualifying income generally includes your wages, salaries, tips, bonuses, commissions and similar amounts. But the following items don't count:

- Pension or annuity income
- Compensation that was deferred from a previous year
- Amounts other than nontaxable combat pay that are excluded from income

Safe harbor. The IRS recognizes that it's unclear whether some items qualify. To make things easy, the IRS says you can rely on your Form W-2. Take the amount in the box labeled "Wages, tips, other compensation" and subtract the amount in the box labeled "Nonqualified plans." You can treat that number as qualified income for your IRA contributions.

Working overseas. People who work overseas can exclude some or all of their wage income if they meet certain requirements. Income that's excluded under this rule can't be used as qualifying income for IRA contributions. Remember, though, there's a special rule for nontaxable combat pay.

> Many people have made the mistake of contributing to an IRA when they had no qualifying income because of the foreign earned income exclusion. The resulting excess contribution incurs a penalty if it isn't corrected in time.

Net earnings from self-employment

Qualifying income also includes types of income that are subject to self-employment tax. (It includes these types of income even if you don't pay self-employment tax because of your religious beliefs.) You may earn self-employment income in various ways:

- You can be an independent contractor (a consultant, for example) providing services without becoming an employee.
- You can be a professional (such as a dentist or an accountant) with your own practice.
- You can have your own business (not in a corporation)—in other words, you can be a sole proprietor. If you're a sole proprietor, you report your business income and deductions on Schedule C of Form 1040.
- You can be a member of a partnership or limited liability company ("LLC") that carries on a trade or business. In this case, the partnership or LLC should provide you with a Schedule K-1 each year telling you how much income to report, and how much of that income (if any) is self-employment income.

Active involvement. In any of these cases your income is self-employment income only if your services are "a material income-producing factor." In plain English, you don't have self-employment income if you're merely an investor. You need to be actively involved in the business that produces the income.

Investment income doesn't count. Even if you're actively involved in a business, you can't include investment income in your qualifying income. For example, if you're a member of a business partnership that maintains some investments on the side, the income produced by the investments isn't qualifying income. If your partnership doesn't have a business other than investing, none of the income is compensation income, even if you're actively involved.

> *Traders.* Income from trading stocks or other securities is not qualifying income, even if you make the "mark-to-market" election, converting your profits to ordinary income.

Net earnings. When figuring how much qualifying income you have to support your IRA contribution, it's your *net* earnings from self-employment that count. Subtract your expenses and other deductions connected with the activity that produced the income. Also, reduce your self-employment income by the amount you contribute to a retirement plan connected with your self-employment (such as a Keogh plan), and by the deduction for one-half of the self-employment tax.

Loss from self-employment. If you have more than one business that produces self-employment income, a loss from one has to be netted against a profit from the other. But you don't have to net a loss from self-employment against earnings you have as an employee when determining how much qualifying income you have. For example, if you work part of the year as an employee making $6,000, then spend the rest of the year being self-employed with a loss of $5,000, your qualifying income is still $6,000.

S corporations. If you own stock in an S corporation, you'll receive a Schedule K-1 similar to the one you would receive as a member of a partnership. But income you receive as a shareholder of an S corporation is not qualifying income. If you are also an employee of the S corporation, your qualifying income includes amounts earned as an employee, as explained earlier.

Alimony income

For purposes of supporting an IRA contribution, taxable alimony income counts as qualifying income. This special rule permits you to build retirement savings in an IRA even if you don't work as an employee or have self-employment earnings. The rule applies only to taxable alimony income, though. Nontaxable items such as child support are not qualifying income.

Relying on your spouse's income

If you file jointly with a spouse who has qualifying income, you don't need qualifying income of your own. Solely for this purpose you're treated as if you had qualifying income equal to:

- Your qualifying income (if any), plus
- Your spouse's qualifying income, minus
- Your spouse's contributions to traditional IRAs and Roth IRAs.

Of course this rule doesn't get you out of the other requirements. In particular, if the amount of income on your joint return is too high, your contribution limit will be reduced even if your spouse earned all the income.

> You can't rely on your spouse's income to support a contribution to an IRA if you don't file jointly. This is true even if you live in a community property state.

Q: Does my spouse have to make the contribution?

A: Some of the explanations of this rule would lead you to believe the contribution has to come from the spouse with the compensation income. That's not necessary. You can use your own money to make your IRA contribution, even if you're relying on your spouse's qualifying income.

Q: Does this mean I have a spousal IRA?

A: Some people, including the IRS, say you have a spousal IRA when you rely on your spouse's income to support contributions to an IRA. The term seems to suggest there might be special rules that apply to the IRA afterward. That's not the case. Going forward you have exactly the same ownership rights and exactly the same tax treatment as if you relied on your own income to support the IRA contributions. There's no special category of IRA known as a spousal IRA.

> The heading for this provision in the tax law uses the term *spousal IRA* but the term has no independent significance.

Nontaxable combat pay

Combat pay received by members of the armed forces can be tax-free. That's good, but before 2006 it created a problem for retirement savings. As a general rule, qualifying income has to be *taxable* income. Recipients of nontaxable combat pay were not allowed to contribute to IRAs unless they had other qualifying income.

Congress eliminated this problem in 2006. Nontaxable combat pay is now qualified income that can support an IRA contribution. The amount should appear in box 12 of Form W-2 with code Q.

Differential wage payments

Some employers provide payments to employees during military service representing some or all of the wages that would have been paid if the individual were working for the employer. Beginning in 2009, these *differential wage payments* are treated as qualifying income that can support an IRA contribution.

Household chores

Many people would like to set up Roth IRAs for their minor children. The long-term benefit can be huge, as investment earnings remain free of tax for many decades. Contributions aren't allowed, though, if the child doesn't have qualifying income.

You may face the same problem with an older relative. There's no age limit for contributions to a Roth IRA, and the minimum distribution rules don't apply during the lifetime of the original owner. Money stashed in one of these accounts can be left to grandchildren, providing a lasting benefit. But there's no way to do this if the grandparent is a retiree with no qualifying income.

So how do you create qualifying income? Some experts have suggested you can do this by paying family members for household chores. I disagree. If the payment is excessive, or doesn't relate to work actually performed, it can't be considered qualifying income. And there's another problem, even if we eliminate these obvious issues.

Let's say you hire your able-bodied teenager for household chores, and make some favorable assumptions:

- The child is actually doing work for the money.
- You're paying only a reasonable hourly rate for the work.
- You have good records to prove that the work was done and the money paid.

Will that do the trick? Strangely enough, there's no guidance on this issue, but the answer seems clear enough to me. Payments to family members for household chores are not taxable income, so they can't be used to support contributions to IRAs.

It's difficult to *prove* this income isn't taxable. The Internal Revenue Code says all income is taxable unless an exception is made, and there's no exception for amounts paid to family members for household chores. Yet this is one of those things we all know instinctively. No one ever reports this kind of income on a tax return, and no one thinks they're cheating when they fail to do so. The IRS has never suggested that this income should be reported. Just imagine the uproar if the IRS tried to collect tax on the money parents pay their children to babysit younger siblings or mow the lawn.

The leading authority on issues of this kind, the late Boris Bittker, had this to say on the subject:

> "Intrafamily transfers of this type can be properly viewed as excludable by a higher authority than the language of [the Internal Revenue Code]—a supposition, so obvious that it does not require explicit mention in the Code, that Congress never intended to tax them."

As usual, Professor Bittker got it exactly right. The income isn't taxable, and that means it isn't qualifying income that will support an IRA contribution.

Income from a parent's business

It's a different story if you have a business and employ your child (or your parent or grandparent) as a way of satisfying the requirement for qualifying income. Many parents used this approach even before Congress created the Roth IRA, partly for the practical advantages (save on recruiting costs!) and partly because it allows parents to claim a business deduction while keeping the money in the family.

There are a number of cases where the IRS challenged these deductions, especially when payments went to very young children or the amount paid seemed to be out of line with the fair value of a child's services. The Tax Court has taken a balanced approach, siding with the taxpayers when it appeared they paid reasonable compensation for work that was actually performed, but denying the deduction when the facts indicated otherwise.

15

Income Limitation for Roth IRA Contributions

If your income is too high, your Roth IRA contribution limit may be reduced.

ALTHOUGH CONGRESS ABOLISHED THE INCOME LIMIT on Roth conversions as of 2010, the income limit for contributions remains in place. This rule reduces the amount you can contribute to a Roth IRA for any year your income is above certain levels. This rule *does not* apply to Roth 401k or similar accounts. Also, this rule applies only to regular contributions to a Roth IRA: it doesn't affect rollovers or conversions. As discussed later, most people affected by this rule can get around it by contributing to a traditional IRA and then using a conversion to move that money to a Roth.

This rule applies based on two factors: your filing status and your *modified adjusted gross income* ("modified AGI"). Here's how it works:

- If your modified AGI is below the level specified for your filing status, you can ignore this rule (but you still have to meet other requirements, such as having enough qualifying income).
- If your modified AGI is above that level, but not too much higher, you can still contribute to a Roth IRA, but your contribution limit will be reduced.
- When your modified AGI reaches an upper limit, you can't contribute to a Roth IRA at all.

When this rule applies to reduce or eliminate your ability to contribute to a Roth IRA, you can make contributions to a traditional IRA to make up the difference. For example, if your overall limit is $5,500, but this rule reduces your Roth IRA contribution by 40%, you can put $3,000 in a Roth IRA and another $2,000 in a traditional IRA.

Who's affected

You're only affected by these rules if your modified adjusted gross income is above certain levels. Those levels depend on your filing status, and they are adjusted each year for inflation. Here are the numbers for 2015. Numbers for other years are available at Fairmark.com in the Reference Room.

- **Single:** If you're not married, your contribution limit will be reduced when your modified AGI exceeds $116,000 for 2015. It's completely eliminated when your modified AGI is $15,000 above that level.
- **Married filing jointly:** If you're married and file a joint return with your spouse, your contribution limit will be

reduced when your joint modified AGI exceeds $183,000 for 2015, and completely eliminated when your joint modified AGI is $10,000 above that level.

- **Married filing separately, living apart:** If you're married and file a separate return, and live apart from your spouse at all times during the year, apply the same rule as if you were single.
- **Married filing separately, other:** If you're married and file a separate return, and live with your spouse at any time during the year, your contribution limit will be reduced when your modified AGI exceeds $0, and completely eliminated when your modified AGI reaches $10,000. Considering that few people with income below $10,000 are able to add to their retirement savings, this rule effectively bars contributions by nearly all people who are married filing separately.

You may have noticed a strange quirk in these rules: once you reach the level where your Roth IRA contribution begins to be reduced, it takes only $10,000 of additional income to make you completely ineligible if you're a joint filer, but the number is $15,000 for singles. It might seem logical to have this benefit phase out more slowly for married couples than for singles, but the law provides just the reverse.

Modified AGI

This limit applies when your *modified AGI* is too high. Finding your modified AGI is a two-step process: first find your adjusted gross income, then apply the modifications.

AGI. Adjusted gross income ("AGI") represents your total income reduced by certain deductions known as "adjustments," but before you take your itemized deductions or standard deduction, and before you take the deduction for your exemptions.

If you file regular Form 1040 or Form 1040A, adjusted gross income is the last number at the bottom of page 1 (and the first number at the top of page 2). On Form 1040EZ, adjusted gross income appears on line 4.

Q: Are capital gains included in AGI?

A: Yes. For example, if you have a $20,000 capital gain, it will increase your AGI (and your modified AGI) by $20,000. This is true even for long-term capital gains that are subject to special tax rates.

Modifications. To arrive at your modified AGI, start with your adjusted gross income, subtract any income from Roth conversions, and then add back the following items:

- Any deduction you claimed for a regular (non-rollover) contribution to a traditional IRA.
- Any deduction you claimed for interest on education loans or for qualified tuition and related expenses.
- Any income you excluded because of the foreign earned income exclusion.
- Any exclusion or deduction you claimed for foreign housing.
- Any interest income from series EE bonds that you were able to exclude because you paid qualified higher education expenses.
- Any amount you excluded as employer-paid adoption expense.
- Any amount claimed as a domestic production activities deduction.

Note that although you add back contributions to a traditional IRA, you are not required to add back any contribution you made to an employer plan such as a 401k plan. If you are running up against the limit for modified AGI, one way to reduce that number is to make deductible contributions to an employer plan.

Remember, income from a Roth IRA conversion is not included in modified AGI, so a conversion will not interfere with your ability to make a regular contribution.

> **Example:** You're single and have a traditional IRA worth $120,000 with no basis. Before you decide to make a conversion your modified AGI is $80,000. If you convert this IRA to a Roth your AGI will increase to $200,000, but your *modified* AGI remains unchanged at $80,000, so you can still make contributions to your Roth IRA.

Proportionate reduction

The dollar limit on Roth IRA contributions declines gradually as your income rises above the level specified for your filing status. For married taxpayers, other than those who file separately *and* live separately, the relevant range of income is $10,000. That means your permitted contribution is reduced 1% for every $100 of income above the specified dollar amount.

> **Example:** You're married filing jointly and your modified AGI is $4,000 above the level specified for your filing status. Your permitted contribution is reduced by 40%.

The rule works the same way for singles (and married taxpayers who file separately and live separately) except their limit is phased out over a $15,000 range of income. Your permitted contribution is reduced 1% for every $150 of income above the specified dollar amount.

> **Example:** You're single and your modified AGI is $3,000 above the level specified for your filing status. Your permitted contribution is reduced by 20%.

Special rules

There are two special rules for figuring the permitted contribution to a Roth IRA:

- If the limit doesn't work out to an even $10 increment, it's rounded up to the next higher $10 increment. For example, if the math says your limit should be $1371.50, this rule sets your limit at $1,380.
- Your limit isn't reduced below $200 until your modified AGI reaches the level where the limit is completely eliminated. For example, if the math says your limit should be $50, you can still contribute $200.

Exceeding the limit

A contribution that seemed okay when you made it can end up violating this rule because of a change in filing status or an unexpected increase in income. The result would be an *excess contribution.* Chapter 20 explains how to deal with this situation.

Avoiding the rule

If the income limitation prevents you from contributing to a Roth IRA, you may be able to work around the problem by making a "back door" contribution as described in the next chapter.

16

Backdoor Roth IRA Contributions

There's an income limitation for Roth IRA contributions but not for conversions, so a conversion may let you bring a contribution in through the back door.

CONGRESS MADE A PECULIAR CHOICE, eliminating the income limitation for Roth conversions while leaving it in place for Roth IRA contributions. Under these rules, someone who wants to contribute to a Roth IRA but has too much income may be able to accomplish a similar result by contributing to a traditional IRA and then converting that amount to a Roth. This technique, which has come to be known as the *backdoor* Roth IRA contribution, can be effective in the right situation, but it isn't quite as simple as it sounds.

> There are two versions of this technique: one where the contribution to the traditional IRA is deductible and one where it is not.

Over age 70½

Before we begin, let's note that this technique isn't for everyone. In particular, it doesn't apply to individuals over the age of 70½. There's no age limitation on contributions to Roth IRAs, but a backdoor contribution requires you to make a contribution to a *traditional* IRA, and the age limitation *does* apply there, even if your ultimate destination is a Roth. Once you reach that age, your contributions have to enter through the front door or not at all.

Deductible contribution

We rarely see anyone use the backdoor method when they can make a deductible contribution to a traditional IRA, but it's a possible choice. Suppose all of the following are true:

- You're eligible to make a deductible contribution to a traditional IRA;
- You prefer to make a nondeductible contribution to a Roth IRA; but
- You aren't eligible to contribute to a Roth IRA because of the income limitation.

In this situation, it would be perfectly acceptable to (a) make a deductible contribution to a traditional IRA, and (b) make a taxable conversion of that amount to a Roth IRA. The income from the conversion is offset by the deduction, so you come out more or less where you would be if you had been allowed to contribute the money directly to the Roth. See the caveat below about withdrawals, however.

We don't see this very often for a couple of reasons. First, if you participate in an employer plan, you lose the ability to deduct contributions to traditional IRAs at a lower income level than where you lose the ability to contribute to a Roth IRA. So this version of the backdoor Roth doesn't apply if you participate in an employer plan.

The other hangup is that when your income is high enough to disqualify you from a Roth contribution, you're likely to be in at least the 28% tax bracket (though this isn't necessarily the case). While a Roth contribution can be desirable for someone in that bracket, few people realize this, so they're likely to leave the money in the traditional IRA to retain the tax benefit of deducting the contribution.

Nondeductible contribution, no existing TIRA

The backdoor technique is more often used by people who are unable to deduct a contribution to a traditional IRA. The potential payoff is greater here: your contribution isn't going to produce a deduction anyway, so you'd much rather have it go into a Roth, where the investment earnings will eventually be tax-free, than a traditional IRA, where you merely postpone taxation of the investment earnings.

This approach works best for people who don't have an existing traditional IRA. You would create a new traditional IRA and make a nondeductible contribution, then convert it to a Roth. You would pay no tax on the conversion unless the account produced earnings during the small interval of time between the contribution to the traditional IRA and conversion to a Roth. That means the tax consequences are pretty much the same as if you had been allowed to contribute directly to the Roth.

From this perspective, it kind of makes you wonder why Congress didn't eliminate the income limitation on Roth contributions at the same time as the income limitation on conversions.

Backdoor for TIRA owners

Things get more complicated if you already have a traditional IRA. This is because of the infamous *aggregation rule.* When you take money from a traditional IRA, whether it's a regular withdrawal or a conversion, you determine the tax consequences by treating all your traditional IRAs as if they were one big IRA. This means you may have to pay tax on the Roth conversion when using the backdoor method, even if the account you're converting has never had any deductible contributions or investment earnings.

> **Example:** You have a $20,000 traditional IRA from an earlier 401k rollover, and all the money in that account is pre-tax. You want to make a $5,000 backdoor Roth contribution, so you set up a new traditional IRA, contribute $5,000, and convert it to a Roth the next day.

You have to add all your traditional IRAs together to figure the tax consequences of the conversion. You have $20,000 of pre-tax money in one IRA and $5,000 of after-tax money in the other. That makes a total of $25,000, and 80% of that amount is pre-tax. Result: when you convert $5,000 you pay tax on 80% of that amount, or $4,000. This isn't a complete disaster, because it also means you now have $4,000 of basis in your traditional IRA that will eventually come out tax-free. It's probably not the result you intend, though.

The actual tax cost will depend on the aggregate size of your traditional IRAs and how much if any consists of after-tax dollars.

Some people are able to solve this problem with an IRA-to-401k rollover. See *Isolating IRA basis* in Chapter 25.

Just so we're clear

Some people have the idea that the income limitation is what prevents them from *starting* a Roth IRA, and figure that once they have their foot in the door they can make regular Roth contributions in subsequent years. Au contraire, mon frère. Until your modified adjusted gross income falls into the range that permits an annual Roth contribution, the back door is the only one open to you.

Here's another point to keep in mind. When we talk about the rules for taking money out of your Roth IRA, we'll see that you can withdraw regular contributions at any time, free of tax or penalty. The backdoor approach means your money is coming into the Roth IRA by way of a conversion, not a regular contribution, so different rules apply. In particular, if any part of the conversion was taxable, then a withdrawal of those dollars (the ones that were taxable) before age 59½ could lead to a 10% penalty unless they sat in the Roth at least five years before you pulled them out.

One more little point. There is no required waiting period between the date you contribute to a traditional IRA and the date you convert it to a Roth. I recommend that you obtain positive confirmation that the money was deposited in a traditional IRA before converting it to a Roth, and in any event do the conversion at least a day later than the contribution so there is a paper trail establishing that you performed both of the required steps. You don't want to leave open the possibility for the IRS to argue that the money never settled in the traditional IRA, causing it to be treated as a regular (and unpermitted) contribution to a Roth.

Possible legal challenge?

Some tax professionals have raised the possibility that the IRS could challenge the tax treatment of the backdoor Roth technique. Their concern is that the IRS may collapse the two transactions (a contribution to a traditional IRA followed by a conversion) into one (a contribution to a Roth, which is not permitted because of the income limit). In this case you could incur a penalty for making an excess contribution to the Roth.

My assessment: there is no cause for concern. It would have been obvious to the taxwriters in Congress that they were creating this opportunity when they eliminated the income limit on conversions, and they chose not to block it. As a result, there is a fair argument to be made that Congress intentionally created this opportunity. What's more, the IRS has known about this technique since before the law eliminating the income limit on conversions took effect, and has not lifted a finger to stop it. Leading mutual fund provider Vanguard Group recommends the technique and reports processing some $100 million in backdoor Roth contributions in 2013.

I doubt that anything will be done to block this technique. It's more likely that Congress will remove the income limitation on Roth IRA contributions, doing away with the need to take these steps. In the unlikely event that Congress or the IRS decides to block these transactions, the change will be prospective only. People who have already done backdoor contributions will not be penalized.

> As a reminder, I *do* recommend making sure the two transactions are distinct: obtain confirmation that the contribution to the traditional IRA has been documented before proceeding with the conversion, and avoid doing both transactions on the same day.

17

Roth Accounts in 401k and Similar Plans

Your contributions to a 401k or similar plan can go to a Roth account if you work for an employer that offers this option.

GETTING STARTED WITH ROTH SAVINGS in an employer plan isn't hard. Here are the requirements:

- You need to work for an employer that offers this kind of account.
- You need to meet the requirements for participation in the plan.
- Using a form supplied by your employer, you need to establish your contribution amount and indicate that your contributions should go to a Roth account.

Some companies make it even easier: they may automatically start your contributions as soon as you qualify for the plan. The only thing you have to do then is make sure the contributions go into a Roth account, if that's what you want.

Availability of Roth accounts

The Roth IRA has been with us since 1998, but Roth accounts in employer plans weren't permitted until 2006. The original law creating these accounts applied only to 401k and 403b plans and had a sunset date, meaning the law could expire. In 2006 Congress passed another law making Roth accounts in these plans permanent. Arrangements offered by state and local governments, known as 457b plans, were added in 2011, and the federal government's Thrift Savings Plan began offering Roth accounts in 2012.

Employers are not required to offer these accounts, however. Some don't want to incur the costs involved in setting up and maintaining Roth accounts in their retirement plans until it's clear employees will appreciate the benefit. If your employer offers a 401k, 403b or 457b plan but does not yet offer this feature, make your interest known.

Meeting participation requirements

Your employer will let you know when you have met the requirements to participate in the company's retirement plan. There are no separate requirements for Roth accounts. Everyone who can contribute to the plan is allowed to use Roth accounts if the plan includes this feature.

Q: What about income limits or filing status?

A: These don't matter for Roth accounts in employer plans. If you participate in a plan that offers this feature, you're free to take advantage.

Designating contributions

Your contributions won't necessarily end up in a Roth account just because your employer's retirement plan offers this feature. Some companies may set up their plan to make a Roth account the default choice, but otherwise you have to *choose* to put your contributions in a Roth account. You'll make this choice on a form supplied by your employer.

Now or never. Once the money goes into one kind of account you can't change your mind and say you want it switched to the other kind. You're allowed to change where your *future* contributions will go at any time your company's plan allows you to make other changes in your contributions. (By law you can do this at least once a year, but most companies allow you to change your contributions more often.) Past contributions cannot be changed from one type of account to the other.

> This is a big difference from Roth IRAs, where you can use the recharacterization rules to switch your contributions from Roth to traditional or vice versa until October 15 of the year after the year for which you made the contribution.

Contribution limit

Your *elective deferrals* for any given year cannot exceed an overall dollar limit. For 2015 the numbers are $18,000 for younger workers and $24,000 for those who are 50 or older. This is a global limit that applies to the total of all your elective deferrals in a given year to all plans that permit this type of contribution, including 401k plans, 403b plans, salary reduction SEPs, SIMPLEs, the federal Thrift Savings Plan, 457b plans and 501(c)(18) plans. If you participate in more than one of these plans, the amount you contribute to one reduces the amount you're allowed to contribute to any other.

For purposes of this rule, Roth contributions are considered "elective deferrals" even though they don't reduce your taxable income. You can contribute to traditional and Roth accounts in the same year, but the total of all these contributions has to stay within the same overall limit. If you contribute $5,000 to a traditional 401k account, the amount you can contribute to a Roth 401k account for the same year is reduced by $5,000.

The people running the retirement plan should have procedures in place to prevent you from going over the limit for contributions to that plan. Mistakes of this kind can happen, but they tend to be rare. It's not at all unusual, however, to see someone exceed this limit when working for more than one employer in the same year. A plan administrator is not responsible for finding out the amount you contributed to another employer's plan and keeping your total elective deferrals within the limit. That's *your* responsibility. If you aren't careful, you can go over the limit.

> **Example:** During the first six months of the year you contribute $2,500 per month to your 401k account. Then you take a job at another company, sign up for their 401k plan and contribute $2,500 per month to the *new* 401k account for the *last* six months of the year.

Your total elective deferrals for the year are $30,000. That's over the limit, and that means you have a problem. Unless you can get a corrective distribution by April 15 of the next year you'll end up with highly unfavorable tax consequences. See Chapter 20 for details.

Certain other rules for these plans may prevent you from contributing the full amount, or even force the plan to return a portion of your contributions. Responsibility for these rules lies with the plan administrator, not the participant, so we won't discuss them here.

Matching contributions

Many employers offer matching contributions to encourage workers to save in their retirement accounts. That's a great way to turbocharge your retirement savings. Contributions to a Roth account are eligible for the same matching money as contributions to traditional accounts. Of course this doesn't mean you can double up: if your employer matches the first $6,000 of contributions, you won't expand that amount by contributing to both types of accounts.

Match goes to traditional account. If you're saving in a Roth account, it might seem logical to get your matching money in the same account. That doesn't happen, though, and for a simple reason: you don't pay tax on the matching contribution until you take it out of the account. If the matching contribution went into a Roth account, it's possible you'd never pay tax on that money at all. Congress didn't want to be quite that generous, so the law says your matching contributions have to go into a traditional account.

> **Example:** Your employer offers a Roth 401k and makes a matching contribution of 25 cents for every dollar you put in the 401k, up to $6,000. You decide to contribute $500 per month to take full advantage of the match, and you check the box indicating your contributions should go into a Roth account. At the end of the year, you'll have $6,000 in a Roth account and $1,500 in a traditional

account, subject to adjustments for investment performance.

> It's perfectly okay that you have both kinds of accounts, with the matching money going into a traditional account. Having your money split between both types of accounts may work to your advantage, providing more flexibility for planning when you're ready to take distributions.

You can use an in-plan conversion to move matching dollars (and other pre-tax amounts) to the Roth portion of your 401k or similar account if your employer has set up its retirement plan to permit this type of transaction. You would have to report this amount as taxable income for the year of the move, however. See *In-plan conversion* in Chapter 21.

18

Retirement Savings Contributions Credit

For people who qualify, this tax credit is almost like getting a matching contribution from the government.

PEOPLE WITH LOW TO MODERATE INCOME often find it hard to save for retirement, so there's a special tax credit designed to help this group. If you qualify, and contribute to a retirement account, Uncle Sam will provide a tax credit that can be as much as half the amount you contributed. You can claim this credit even if you received matching contributions from your employer!

> This is a credit, not a deduction. When you deduct $100, your savings depend on your tax bracket (for example, $15 in the 15% bracket). When you have a $100 credit, your tax goes down by the full amount, $100.

Example: You contribute $1,000 to your company's 401k plan and get a matching contribution of $500, so you have a total of $1,500 in your account. If you qualify for the highest level of this credit, you get a $500 reduction in your taxes, so it cost you only $500 to add $1,500 to your retirement savings.

> Initially this credit was a temporary measure, but Congress made it permanent in 2006.

On your own

Congress didn't want to allow this credit for minors, full-time students or dependents. You're disqualified if any of the following are true for the year you want to claim the credit:

- You were less than 18 years of age at the end of the year. (If you were born on January 1, you're considered 18 as of the day before your 18th birthday, on December 31 of the preceding year, for purposes of this rule.)
- You were a full time student. For this purpose, you're considered a full-time student if, during some part of five calendar months, you were enrolled for the number of hours or courses your school considers full-time.
- Someone else claims an exemption for you on their tax return.

In any of these situations you may be eligible to make retirement savings contributions, and it may be a good idea for you to do so, but you won't qualify for the credit.

Income limits

There are income limits for this credit. They depend on your filing status and are adjusted each year for inflation. For 2015, if your filing status is single or married filing separately you receive a 50% credit with income up to $18,250, a 20% credit with income over that level up to $19,750, and a 10% credit with income over that level up to $30,500. If you file as a head of household your income limits are 1½ times those figures, and for a married couple filing jointly they're double those figures. Updated numbers are posted in the Reference Room at Fairmark.com as they become available.

For example, if you're married filing jointly with income of $45,000, your credit will be 10% of the amount contributed, up to the limit described below. But if your joint income is $36,500 or less, the credit will be half the amount contributed.

Income. For this purpose, we're talking about your adjusted gross income, which is your income after taking certain deductions (such as a deduction for your contribution to a traditional IRA), but before claiming personal exemptions, itemized deductions or the standard deduction. If you excluded income from foreign sources, you'll have to add that back when figuring this credit.

> These rules create a cliff effect where a single dollar of added income can reduce the size of the credit by hundreds of dollars. If you find this is true when preparing your tax return, you may be able to avoid that result by making a deductible contribution to a traditional IRA.

Eligible contributions

What types of retirement contributions qualify? Plenty. You can put money into any of the following:

- A traditional or Roth IRA
- A traditional or Roth account in a 401k or 403b plan
- A governmental 457b plan

- A SIMPLE IRA plan or salary reduction SEP
- A 501(c)(18) plan

You can also count after-tax employee contributions to a qualified retirement plan, but only if the contributions are voluntary. In all cases, your contribution has to be "new money." Rollover contributions don't count.

Maximum amount. The maximum contribution amount for this credit is $2,000 per person. For example, if you contribute $3,000 and qualify for the 10% credit, your credit will be $200 because only the first $2,000 of contributions count. This limit applies after the reduction for distributions described next.

Reduction for distributions

The idea behind the credit is to help you build retirement savings, so the credit doesn't apply unless you're putting more money into your retirement savings than you're taking out. When you figure the credit you have to reduce your eligible contributions by the amount of distributions you received during a "testing period" consisting of the year for which you're claiming the credit, the period after the end of that year until the due date (including extensions) of your tax return for that year, and the two years before that year.

> **Example:** You contributed $4,000 to an IRA this year, but you took a $2,500 distribution from a retirement plan two years ago. Only $1,500 of your contribution is potentially eligible for the credit.

Certain types of distributions don't count:

- Distributions that are rolled over to another retirement plan or converted to a Roth IRA
- Corrective distributions

- Loans from a 401k or other employer plan that are treated as distributions (usually because of failure to repay the loan)
- Distributions from military retirement plans

If you file jointly with a spouse who took retirement plan distributions, you may also have to reduce your contributions by those distributions when figuring the credit. Bottom line: check these rules carefully if you or your spouse took any distributions from retirement plans during the testing period.

Credit is limited to tax

This is a "nonrefundable" credit. That means you can't use it to get a refund that's bigger than the amount you paid in the form of withholding or estimated tax payments. In other words, if you're already paying zero tax, you can't use this credit to pay less than zero. However, you can use the credit to increase the amount of your refund, if it isn't as big as the amount that was withheld.

> **Example:** Your total income tax withholding for the year was $800, and before you figure this credit you're expecting a refund of $500. That means you can't claim more than $300 credit (boosting your refund to $800, the amount of your withholding) even if you would otherwise qualify for a larger credit.

19

Retroactive Switching

You can change your mind about the type of IRA used for a contribution, switching it to the other type retroactively.

YOU MIGHT CALL IT THE "OOPS" RULE. You can switch a regular contribution from one type of IRA to another: from a Roth to a traditional IRA or from a traditional IRA to a Roth. You can use this rule to recover from a mistake, or to benefit from a stock market swing, or simply because you changed your mind.

Recharacterization

To do this you would use the *recharacterization* rules. Most people tend to think of these rules only in connection with Roth conversions. (We'll cover that aspect in Chapter 23.) Yet a recharacterization can also be used to switch a regular contribution from one type of IRA to the other. The switch has retroactive effect: you'll be treated as if your original contribution went to the new IRA. In short, it's a do-over.

You may not be able to erase all aspects of your previous decision. This rule doesn't allow you to recover fees you may have incurred in connection with the original action. In fact, your IRA provider may charge a fee to cover the paperwork of the recharacterization. And a recharacterization doesn't undo the results of an unfortunate investment. This is an almost magical way to undo the *tax* consequences of an earlier action, but that's as far as it goes.

> The money or other assets you transfer in a recharacterization will be adjusted for investment performance as described later.

How it works

A recharacterization moves money from one type of IRA to another. You can't do a rollover-type of transfer, where you take money out of one IRA and, within 60 days, transfer it into another. That means you have just two possible ways to accomplish a recharacterization:

- Transfer the money or other assets from one type of IRA to another while keeping it at the same IRA provider.
- Move the money or other assets directly from one IRA provider to another (a trustee-to-trustee transfer), with the money going into a different type of IRA.

The first method is usually easier because it involves just one IRA provider. You'll fill out whatever form they provide, telling them what you want to do, and they'll take care of the rest. Even if you plan to move the money to a different IRA provider, it might be easier to do the recharacterization at the first one and then move the money in a rollover or trustee-to-trustee transfer. You can combine a recharacterization with a transfer to a different trustee if that approach happens to fit your situation, but it requires you to coordinate the actions of two IRA providers that may or may not play well together.

> In either case, follow up afterward to make certain the recharacterization took place as you intended. The IRS determines your tax consequences based on what the IRA provider actually did, not what you *told* them to do.

Possible uses

Here are some of the possible ways you could use this rule:

- *Regular contribution to traditional IRA.* You made a regular contribution to a traditional IRA and now you wish you had contributed that money to a Roth instead. No problem! Substitute a Roth IRA for the traditional IRA as the recipient of that contribution.
- *Regular contribution to a Roth IRA.* The same thing works in the other direction. Maybe you found out your income was too high for the contribution to the Roth IRA, or you simply changed your mind about which type of IRA will work best for you. Whatever the reason, you can substitute a traditional IRA for the Roth, and you'll be treated as if the contribution originally went to the traditional IRA.
- *Investment performance.* You might want to make a switch if the investments in your account move sharply higher after a contribution to a traditional account, or sharply lower after a contribution to a Roth.

Example: You chose a Roth account for your $5,000 contribution, but happened to hit some terrible luck, and six months later the account was worth $3,000. If you're eligible for a deductible contribution to a traditional IRA, you might want to recharacterize your contribution. You would be moving only $3,000 to the TIRA, but you would be treated as if you contributed $5,000. Afterward you can convert back to a Roth, paying tax on the $3,000 value. You save tax on $2,000 and end up in the same place as if you simply left the money in the Roth account.

Q: What if I want to move just part of a contribution?

A: No problem. Recharacterization is not an all-or-nothing proposition. However, you have to move earnings related to whatever portion of the contribution you're moving.

Q: Can I specify which contribution is being recharacterized?

A: Yes. For example, if you did one contribution in January and another in June, you can switch the June contribution while leaving the January contribution in place, even if both went into the same Roth IRA. You might want to do this if you had strong investment performance between January and June, for example.

Recharacterization not allowed

Some types of contributions aren't eligible for this treatment.

- *Tax-free transactions.* If you made a tax-free rollover or trustee-to-trustee transfer to a traditional IRA, you can't use the recharacterization rules to transform that event into a conversion.
- *Employer contributions.* You can't use this rule to switch an employer contribution from a SEP IRA or SIMPLE IRA into a Roth IRA.
- *Salary reduction contributions.* The recharacterization rule doesn't apply to salary reduction contributions to 401k or similar plans. You're stuck with whatever choice you made at the time of the contribution (Roth account or traditional).

> Let's be clear about what this means. Subject to restrictions explained in Part IV, you *are* allowed to convert a traditional employer account to a Roth account. You can also use the recharacterization rules to undo such a conversion. The thing you *can't* do is use the recharacterization rules to change the place where an employer contribution or salary reduction contribution went in the first place.

It's possible to make regular IRA contributions to a SEP IRA. These would be contributions *other than* salary reduction contributions, subject to the same rules that apply to regular contributions to traditional IRAs. If you make that kind of contribution to a SEP IRA, you should be able to use the recharacterization rules to redirect that money to a Roth because that's not an employer contribution.

Q: Suppose I made a contribution, and afterward I did a rollover. Can I still do a recharacterization? Do I have to involve the IRA provider that received the contribution?

A: Yes, you can still do a recharacterization (assuming you're still inside the time limit), and no you don't have to involve the earlier trustee.

Q: Suppose I use these rules to switch a contribution and later change my mind. Can I undo a recharacterization?

A: *No!* Once you've done a recharacterization you're stuck with that decision. If you used this rule to switch from a Roth to a traditional account, you can use a conversion to get back to a Roth. But you can't reinstate the original Roth contribution.

When to act

Generally you can recharacterize a contribution until October 15 of the year in which you file your tax return for the year to which the contribution relates. Bear in mind that an IRA contribution made by April 15 can relate to the previous year.

Example: You make an IRA contribution in March of this year. If you designate it as a contribution for the previous year, your deadline for recharacterizing the contribution is October 15 of the current year. If you designate it as a contribution for the current year, you have until October 15 of *next* year to recharacterize the contribution.

Leave plenty of time. It isn't enough for you to take action within this time limit. Your trustee has to complete the transfer before the deadline. It's best to take action well in advance so there's time to follow up and confirm that the trustee finished the paperwork.

Qualifying for the October 15 deadline. Strictly speaking, the deadline for recharacterizations is the due date of your return, with extensions. Filing for an extension (Form 4868) extends your tax return due date to October 15, and also extends the recharacterization deadline to that date.

But there's also a special procedure that allows you to extend the recharacterization deadline to October 15 even if you filed your return by April 15 without getting an extension. To take advantage, you need to complete the recharacterization by October 15 and file an amended return (Form 1040-X) reflecting any changes required by the recharacterization, including, if necessary, a new or amended Form 8606. Write "Filed pursuant to section 301.9100-2" at the top of the amended return and file it where you filed the original return.

This procedure is available only if you filed your original return by the April 15 deadline. If you slipped up, missing that deadline without filing for an extension, you won't qualify for the six-month extension, and you'll be stuck with an April 15 recharacterization deadline.

Relief after the extended deadline

If you discover a problem after the extended deadline has passed, there's a procedure by which you may be able to obtain permission from the IRS for even later action. You would need to obtain a private letter ruling, however. This is an expensive and time-consuming process that isn't likely to be suitable when dealing with contributions. (Conversions are another story, so we discuss this process in Chapter 23.)

Adjusting for investment performance

When you do a recharacterization, the amount you transfer from one IRA to another has to be adjusted for investment performance during the time it was in the first IRA. If the IRA increased in value, you have to increase the amount of the transfer. A decline in the value of the IRA would mean you transfer a smaller amount.

> **Example:** You start a new Roth IRA with a contribution of $4,000. When you prepare your income tax return for that year, you realize you weren't allowed to make that contribution because of your income level. At that time the account is worth $4,250.

One way to correct this problem is a recharacterization that moves the money to a traditional IRA. (Other possibilities are described in Chapter 20.) Your income level may affect your ability to deduct a contribution to a traditional IRA if you participate in an employer plan, but it won't prevent you from *making* a contribution. If you make this choice, you have to move the entire $4,250 to a traditional IRA.

> It doesn't matter whether the change in the account value represents income (such as dividends or interest) or simply a change in the value of assets, such as stock or mutual fund shares. The only thing that matters is the value of the account.

Moving part of an account. A recharacterization doesn't have to involve the entire balance of an account. Perhaps you're recharacterizing a contribution that put money into an existing IRA that held other assets. Or perhaps you're only recharacterizing part of a contribution. In either case you'll have to adjust the amount you're moving to reflect the investment performance of the IRA during the period the money was in the account.

The adjustment will be based on the overall performance of the IRA during this period. You aren't allowed to use the investment performance of specific assets you acquired when you made this contribution.

The earnings calculation. The basic idea behind the earnings calculation is simple: the amount you're switching will be adjusted by a percentage that represents the percentage change in the IRA that relates to investment performance during the period the money was in the account. The actual calculations can get complicated in some situations, though, so generally you should let your IRA provider figure out the earnings adjustment.

Consequences of switching

When you switch a contribution to a different IRA according to these rules, the new IRA is treated as if it received the contribution in the first place. You'll also treat the new IRA as if it had the earnings (positive or negative) that were actually generated in the old IRA and transferred over when you switched contributions.

> **Example:** You made a $2,000 contribution to a traditional IRA in February of last year. In March of this year you decide you would have been better off with a contribution to a Roth IRA, so you switch the full amount, which at that point is $2,300. Your new Roth IRA is treated as if it received a $2,000 contribution in February of last year and had $300 of earnings, even though this Roth IRA didn't exist when you made the original contribution.

> If a baseball manager decides to bring in a pinch hitter in the middle of an at-bat, the pinch hitter inherits the count of the hitter who was batting. The IRA substitution rule is sort of like that.

Notice that this is a better result than if you did a *conversion* of the traditional IRA, because in that case you would have to pay tax on the $300 of investment earnings.

Transfer before recharacterization

What if you transferred money from one IRA to another before making the recharacterization switch? The rules say you should disregard any tax-free transfers that occur between the date of the original contribution and the date of the recharacterization, provided that you transferred any earnings along with the contribution.

20

Troubleshooting Contributions

How to handle contributions that are too large or not permitted.

A CONTRIBUTION THAT ISN'T PERMITTED, or is larger than permitted, can result in penalties and other undesirable tax consequences. The law provides ways to correct these problems if you act promptly. In some cases you can choose from among two or more methods of correction. This chapter explains how to handle each of the following situations:

- Regular contributions to a Roth IRA that are not permitted, or larger than permitted.
- Excess 401k or 403b contributions.

See Chapter 23 for information about undoing Roth conversions.

Excess Roth IRA contributions

The IRS calls it an *excess contribution* if you contribute too much to a Roth IRA. This includes a situation where you weren't allowed to contribute at all: in this case your permitted contribution is zero, and your contribution is in excess of that amount. An excess contribution can happen in various ways.

- You made a contribution expecting to qualify, but later found that your modified adjusted gross income was too high.
- At the time you made the contribution you expected to have qualifying income later in the year, but that income never materialized.
- You made a contribution up to the limit early in the year, and then (d'oh!) forgot and made another contribution for the same year.

In all of these cases you have an excess contribution. If the excess is not corrected, you'll pay a 6% penalty tax, not just in the year of contribution, but also in each subsequent year the excess remains uncorrected. The penalty tax is imposed on you; that is, it isn't paid out of the IRA, even though it's based on an excess contribution that's held in the IRA.

> **Example:** You made a $4,000 contribution to a Roth IRA in a year when you were not permitted to contribute to a Roth. For the year of the contribution there is no correction, so the 6% penalty applies to the entire $4,000, for a tax of $240. The following year there is a partial correction in the amount of $1,000. The penalty applies to the remaining $3,000, for an additional tax of $180.

If the entire excess remains uncorrected for a number of years, the penalty continues to apply, year after year, to the same amount.

Bear in mind that this penalty applies to the gross amount of the excess, not just to the investment income produced by the excess. If your account produces investment income of 8%, the penalty will be equal to three-fourths of that amount. You have to pay this penalty even if the account produces no investment income at all. If the account loses value, the penalty is limited to 6% of the value remaining as of the end of the year.

> Generally it will be highly undesirable to pay this penalty, although we'll see that in some situations you're better off delaying a correction for one year despite this tax.

Correcting excess Roth IRA contributions

There are four different correction methods potentially available for an excess contribution to a Roth IRA:

- Recharacterize the contribution, with any allocable investment income, to a traditional IRA.
- Take a corrective distribution, with any allocable investment income, by October 15 of the year after you made the excess contribution.
- Take a later distribution, *without* adjustment for investment income, for a correction in a later year.
- Contribute less than the maximum amount allowed in a later year.

These methods have different deadlines and different consequences. The optimal choice in one situation may not be best in other circumstances, or it may not even be available. Let's look at each of these alternatives.

Recharacterization. To recharacterize your contribution you have to move the amount contributed, as adjusted for investment performance, from the Roth IRA to a traditional IRA. Generally you have until October 15 of the year after the contribution to take this action. (See Chapter 19 for details.) If you take this approach, you're treated as if the money went into a traditional IRA in the first place, so the excess is eliminated from the Roth IRA.

This approach is only available if a contribution to a traditional IRA would have been allowed. A recharacterization won't help if you contributed more than the overall IRA contribution limit for the year. Ditto if you failed to generate qualifying income to support your contribution, because this requirement applies to both types of IRA. You also can't use this approach if you were 70½ by the end of the year for which you made the contribution, because contributions to traditional IRAs are not permitted in that case. In all these situations you must look to other corrective measures described later.

A recharacterization will often be the best choice in situations where it is available. It eliminates the penalty tax, and it may even produce a tax deduction. Even if you aren't able to deduct your contribution to a traditional IRA, this solution can work well, especially if you're later able to convert that IRA to a Roth.

Corrective distribution by October 15. Another way to correct an excess contribution is by taking a corrective distribution from the Roth IRA by the due date, with extensions, of the tax return for the year of the contribution. Generally this means you have until October 15 of the year after the year to which the contribution relates. As explained in Chapter 19, you can get an automatic extension of the deadline for a recharacterization until October 15 even if you filed your tax return by April 15 without filing an extension form, but the extra six months is not available if you blew the deadline for filing your tax return without filing the extension form. The same rules apply to the deadline for corrective distributions.

As in the case of a recharacterization, the corrective distribution has to be adjusted for investment performance. This means you'll withdraw a larger amount if the account value grew while the money was in the account. If your investments lost value during that period, you can correct your excess by withdrawing a smaller amount. Generally you'll want to let the IRA provider calculate the income allocation, but if you want to check their math, you can use a worksheet that appears in IRS Publication 590-A.

Any income that's included with the distribution has to be reported on the tax return for the year in which you made the excess contribution. In this case we're looking at the year the money physically went into your IRA, not the year *for which* you made the contribution. It doesn't matter what year the income was *earned* or what year you received the corrective distribution.

> **Example:** You made an excess contribution in December of last year and took a corrective distribution in April of this year. Any income received as part of the corrective distribution has to be reported on last year's income tax return.

Apart from the rule about which year you report the income, it's taxed like any other taxable IRA distribution. If you're under 59½, you'll owe a 10% early distribution penalty on this income unless you happen to qualify for an exception.

> If your excess contribution happened to generate an unusually large amount of investment income before you focused on the need for correction, you might be better off choosing one of the correction methods described below, even if this means paying a 6% penalty on the excess for the year of the contribution.

Later distribution. Once you miss the deadline for a recharacterization or corrective distribution, you're stuck with a 6% penalty for the year of the contribution. But then we have to turn to the next problem: if the excess remains uncorrected, you'll incur *another* 6% penalty. You can avoid this if you take a later distribution. The rules here are not the same as for a corrective distribution:

- To correct an excess for a particular year, you need to take the distribution before the end of that year. You can't wait until the tax return due date for that year.
- In this case you don't have to take any income from the IRA. You simply take an amount equal to the excess contribution.

The second rule can make this method of correcting an excess much easier. In fact, if your account enjoyed particularly strong investment performance after the excess contribution, it might make sense to avoid the first two methods of correction on purpose, even though it means you'll end up paying the 6% penalty tax for the year of the contribution.

> **Example:** You started a Roth IRA in January and put in $4,000, designating it as a contribution for the current year, not the previous year. Fifteen months later, when you prepare your income tax return, you realize you weren't allowed to contribute to a Roth IRA. But there's good news: the investment you made with this money rose in value from $4,000 to $6,000.

To avoid the 6% penalty, you have to take a corrective distribution, including the $2,000 of earnings. You'll pay tax on that $2,000 and, if you're under 59½, you'll pay a 10% early distribution penalty as well. The result could be $700 or more in taxes and penalties.

Instead, you can forget about the corrective distribution. Just take a regular distribution of $4,000 before the end of the second year. This distribution doesn't eliminate the 6% penalty for the year of the contribution, but it eliminates any further 6% penalty. Furthermore, it leaves $2,000 in your Roth IRA, which you may eventually be able to take out tax-free in a qualified distribution. Instead of paying $700 or more and having nothing left in your IRA, you pay $240 and have $2,000 left in your IRA.

Contributing less than the maximum. There's one more way to correct an ongoing excess, and that is simply to contribute less than the amount you would otherwise be allowed to put in your Roth IRA. For example, if you have a $3,000 excess from the previous year, and you're allowed to contribute $5,500 for the current year, you can correct the excess by limiting your contributions to $1,000.

This method is similar to the one just described, where you use regular distributions (not corrective distributions) to correct the excess. You don't avoid the 6% penalty for the year of the contribution, but you can avoid the penalty for future years. And in this case you may not have to take any money out of your IRA at all to achieve the desired result.

> In fact, some people end up correcting an excess without even realizing it. They contribute too much one year, then less than the maximum in a later year, and by the time they figure out what happened the excess is gone, although they owe a 6% penalty tax for at least one year.

Excess deferrals (401k and similar plans)

Most people don't have to worry about contributing too much to their 401k or similar account. Employers maintaining these plans generally have procedures in place to prevent you from going over the applicable limits. An excess contribution is still possible, though, especially if you work for more than one employer in the same year.

> **Example:** During the first six months of the year you contribute $2,500 per month to your 401k account. Then you take a job at another company, sign up for their 401k plan and contribute $2,500 per month to the *new* 401k account for the *last* six months of the year.

If you had stayed with the first employer, the 401k plan administrator almost surely would have cut off your contributions when you reached the applicable limit. The new employer isn't responsible for knowing how much you contributed to the 401k at your previous employer, though. The company will follow your instructions, putting $2,500 per month into the account and bringing your total contributions for the year to $30,000, exceeding the dollar limit.

> It's your responsibility, not the company's, to make sure your contributions stay within this limit.

It might seem logical to suppose that the rules for excess 401k or 403b contributions would be similar to the rules for excess IRA contributions. In fact, the rules are completely different. You don't have all the same methods to correct the excess, the deadline for a correction is different, and the consequences of failing to correct are different.

Correcting the excess. We saw earlier that there are four ways to correct an excess contribution to an IRA. There is only one way to correct an excess contribution to a 401k or similar plan: you need to take a corrective distribution. Furthermore, the deadline is April 15 of the following year. An extension to October 15 is not allowed. And here's another unfortunate twist: the law doesn't *require* employers to make these distributions. If your employer won't cooperate, you won't be able to avoid the unpleasant consequences, described below, of having an uncorrected excess.

The corrective distribution must include the dollar amount necessary to bring your contributions within the limit, plus any investment earnings on that extra money for the time it was in your account. Oddly, though, a special rule says the investment earnings paid out with a corrective distribution are treated as wages, not as a retirement plan distribution. As a result, the 10% early distribution penalty won't apply even if you're under 59½.

You can take the corrective distribution from any account. For example, you might start out contributing to a traditional account and later contribute to a Roth account. It might seem logical that the Roth account is where you have the excess, because that's where you made the later contributions that put you over the limit. But you can choose to take the corrective distribution from the traditional account if that seems like better planning. Likewise, when two or more employers are involved, you can take the corrective distribution from the plan where you made the earlier contribution—if you can get the former employer to cooperate. The key is to get your total down to the limit with a distribution from some account by April 15.

> Most employers need a certain amount of lead time to process these payments, so you shouldn't expect to receive a corrective distribution by April 15 if you notify them a day or two before the deadline.

Failure to correct. Some people don't figure out they have excess contributions until it's too late—or have trouble getting their employer to make a corrective distribution. If you're stuck with an uncorrected excess contribution, you're going to pay tax twice on the same amount. Not exactly an elegant result, but that's what the law says.

If your Roth contributions alone aren't over the limit, the rules say any uncorrected excess is in your traditional contributions, even if they came earlier than your Roth contributions. In this situation you have to report the excess contribution as income on your tax return. Even though you paid tax on this amount, you don't get to treat it as an after-tax contribution, and that means you'll pay tax on this amount again when you withdraw it from your 401k account.

> **Example:** Your limit for the year is $18,000. The first part of the year you worked for a company that offered only a traditional 401k, and you contributed $10,000. The second half of the year you worked for a different company and contributed $12,000 to a Roth 401k account.

As described earlier, you're allowed to correct the excess from either account. If you fail to do so, the rules say the excess is in the traditional account.

Your W-2 from the first employer will show your income reduced by $10,000. The rules say you have to report an additional $4,000 of income for the year to eliminate your tax benefit from the excess contribution (see *Reporting*, below). Eventually you'll withdraw this money from your 401k account (or a rollover account) and pay tax on the same amount again.

Excess Roth contributions. Suppose we change the facts above so you contributed to Roth accounts at both employers. Then you would have an uncorrected excess in your Roth contributions. When this happens, you already paid tax on the money once because there is no reduction in income when you contribute to a Roth account. To make sure you pay the piper, the rules put this excess amount in a special category. It's going to be taxable when you take it out of your Roth 401k account, no matter what. In fact, the first dollars that come out of that account are taxable until you've eliminated the excess *and* any earnings on the excess. What's more, these dollars are not eligible for rollover. They're just sitting there as a ticking tax bomb, waiting to go off.

Reporting. If you have an excess contribution to a traditional 401k account you end up with a Form W-2 that doesn't include all your taxable income. That's true whether or not you took a corrective distribution.

> **Example:** You contributed $15,000 to a traditional 401k account at one employer and $15,000 to a Roth account at another employer.

You'll receive a Form W-2 from one employer showing a reduction in your income in the amount of $15,000, your contribution to the traditional 401k account. The other employer will issue a Form W-2 showing the full amount earned, because contributions to a Roth account are not deductible.

If you take a corrective distribution from the Roth account, your contribution to the traditional account is fully deductible and your Form W-2 reflecting this deduction is correct. But if you took the corrective distribution from the traditional account, or you didn't take a corrective distribution by the deadline, the amount reported as wages on the Form W-2 reflecting a $15,000 contribution to the traditional account isn't correct, because only part of that amount is deductible.

In this situation you *do not* have to get a corrected Form W-2. However, you have to report the additional income on Form 1040 (you aren't allowed to file Form 1040A or Form 1040EZ in this situation). Simply add the proper amount to the amount otherwise reported as wages on line 7. Don't worry about having a total there that doesn't match the total of your Forms W-2. The IRS gets excited when line 7 is *smaller* than the total on Forms W-2, but not when it's *larger.*

Part IV
Roth Conversions

21 Roth Conversions

22 Conversion Consequences

23 Recharacterizing Conversions

24 Conversion Strategy Fundamentals

25 Advanced Conversion Strategies

21

Roth Conversions

A conversion moves money from a traditional retirement account to a Roth account.

CHAPTER 10 DISCUSSES THE ADVANTAGES of a Roth conversion. This Part covers all the details: eligibility, consequences and strategies.

Conversions and rollovers

The original idea for getting money or other assets from a traditional retirement account to a Roth was to create a special category of rollover. You would use the same procedures as when you roll assets from one account to another, but special tax rules would apply because you're rolling to a Roth. As an afterthought, Congress said you can simply convert an existing traditional IRA to a Roth, without going through the process of doing an actual rollover, and you'll be treated as if you did one of these special rollovers.

Strictly speaking, that's still the way the law reads. People have come to use the words differently, though. All transactions that move money or other assets from a traditional retirement account to a Roth are called conversions. The terminology could be confusing because it seems to imply that the money or other assets remain in the same account, which has been converted to a Roth. That's not necessarily the case: a conversion can involve a move from one account to another. Even if you convert an entire account without making any other changes, your IRA provider will most likely set up the Roth as a new account, with a different account number from the old one.

> A partial conversion doesn't result in a single account that's partly traditional and partly Roth. Instead, you end up with your money or other assets split between two accounts, one traditional and one Roth.

Conversion methods

If you're eligible to convert a traditional retirement account to a Roth, there are three methods you can use:

- Do a conversion with the assets remaining at your existing IRA provider. This is the simplest and most common method, with the smallest risk of error.
- Make a direct transfer from the existing account to a different firm where you've established a Roth IRA (a "trustee-to-trustee transfer"). This method can provide an advantage when converting from an employer account to a Roth IRA.
- Take a distribution from the traditional account and, within 60 days, contribute the same amount to a Roth. This is the method that presents the most potential problems.

In all three cases, you can convert the entire account or only a portion.

Meeting the deadline

To meet the deadline for a conversion in the current year, you need to have the money or assets distributed from your traditional account by December 31. If you do that, you can complete the conversion by transferring the money or assets to the Roth after the end of the year and still have it count as a conversion for the year of the distribution. This approach may help people who are running up against the deadline for conversion—but be sure you complete the conversion in a timely manner or you'll simply have a large taxable distribution and nothing to show for it.

Eligibility overview

Congress has gradually liberalized the rules for converting Roth IRAs, but we still have to deal with a number of restrictions. Here are the main points:

- Eligibility no longer depends on your income level or filing status.
- You can't convert an IRA inherited from a person other than your spouse, though it appears you can convert an inherited account in a 401k or similar plan.
- You *can* convert a traditional IRA to a Roth IRA even if you made a rollover within the previous 12 months.
- If you're otherwise eligible, you can convert part of a traditional account to a Roth IRA—in other words, conversion is not an all-or-nothing proposition.

- If you have to take a required minimum distribution from your traditional account for a given year, you can't do a conversion until you've satisfied that requirement.
- You're allowed to do a conversion even if you've started taking SEPP distributions (also called "72t distributions") from your traditional IRA, but following the conversion you have to continue taking distributions, according to the same rules, from the Roth IRA.
- If you used the recharacterization rules to undo a conversion, you can't do a new conversion until the year after the original conversion or, if later, 30 days after the recharacterization.

Details concerning each of these points are provided below.

Modified AGI and Filing status

Prior to 2010 you generally couldn't convert a traditional account to a Roth if your modified adjusted gross income was above $100,000 or if you were married filing separately. These rules no longer apply.

> A special rule permitting a delay in reporting income from a conversion applied only in 2010, but elimination of the income and filing status limitations is permanent.

Inherited IRAs

You can't convert an IRA you inherit from a person other than your spouse. There was a brief period in 2008 when this looked like a possibility, but Congress passed a technical correction that eliminated the possibility. (See below for discussion of converting an *employer* account inherited from someone other than a spouse.)

Inheriting from your spouse. If you inherit a traditional IRA from your spouse, you can elect to treat the account as your own. Once you make this election, it's treated the same as an account you created from your own savings, so you can do a conversion according to the usual rules.

Conversion within 12 months of a rollover

Normally you're not permitted to roll an IRA more than once within a 12-month period. This rule applies to Roth IRAs, too, but with a special exception. For purposes of this rule you're permitted to disregard a conversion from a traditional IRA to a Roth IRA, even if you used a rollover-type conversion (where you take money out of the traditional IRA and, within 60 days, contribute it to a Roth IRA).

> **Example:** You withdrew money from your traditional IRA and rolled it to a different traditional IRA within 60 days. Three months later you want to convert this traditional IRA to a Roth IRA. This conversion is permitted if you meet the other requirements—even if you use the rollover method of conversion.

Note that you'll have a problem if you use the rollover method of conversion within 12 months of another rollover and you later want or need to recharacterize the conversion. Recharacterization would turn the conversion into a regular rollover, violating the rule against two such rollovers within 12 months. For safety's sake, whenever possible it's best to make a trustee-to-trustee transfer, avoiding use of the 60-day rollover rule, whether you're converting an IRA or simply moving it to a different provider.

Converting part of your IRA

There's no rule that says you have to convert your entire IRA at once. You can convert part of an IRA if you choose. Unfortunately though, you can't choose to convert only the nontaxable part of a traditional IRA that contains taxable and nontaxable money.

> **Example:** You have a traditional IRA with a balance of $10,000, which includes $6,000 of nondeductible contributions. If you convert $6,000 of this IRA to a Roth IRA, you're required to treat that conversion as coming 60% from nondeductible contributions (the nontaxable part) and 40% from other money (the taxable part). You'll report $2,400 of taxable income, and you'll still have $2,400 of basis in the traditional IRA.

See *Isolating IRA basis* in Chapter 25 for a possible solution to this problem.

Required minimum distributions and conversions

If you have to take a required minimum distribution ("RMD") for a year in which you want to do a conversion, you have to take the RMD *first.* The IRS says the first dollars that come out of a traditional IRA during the year have to be treated as the required distribution, and those dollars aren't eligible for a rollover or conversion. This rule applies in the year you turn 70½, even though you're allowed to postpone the RMD until April 1 of the following year. You have to take an RMD *for* that year even if you don't take it *in* that year, and that means you can't do a conversion that year unless you take the RMD first.

Violating the rule. What happens if you do a conversion without taking the RMD first? The conversion is treated as a distribution from the traditional IRA, so you've satisfied the RMD requirement. That's good, because it means you won't incur the horrible 50% penalty for failing to take the RMD. But the portion of the conversion representing the RMD doesn't qualify for conversion. You're treated as if you took the RMD from the traditional IRA and made a regular (non-conversion) contribution to the Roth. Normally this will result in an excess contribution. See Chapter 20 for corrective measures.

Converting while taking 72t payments

In general, you'll pay a 10% early distribution penalty tax if you take distributions from a traditional IRA before age 59½. One of the exceptions to this rule is for certain "substantially equal periodic payments." These are sometimes called *SEPP* payments or *72t* payments.

> Don't confuse 72t payments with required minimum distributions, which are discussed above. Both involve annual distributions from a retirement account, but they serve different purposes and have different rules.

We won't go through all the rules for 72t payments here. The rule that's important for present purposes is one that says your periodic payments must continue for at least five years or, if later, until you're age 59½ or disabled. If you don't continue to receive payments according to the method you originally chose, you'll be stuck with penalties—not just for the year you changed your payments, but also for all the past years in which you avoided penalties under this rule.

Example: You began receiving 72t payments when you were 47. Four years later you decide you need to withdraw the entire remaining balance of your IRA. The 10% penalty applies to all of your withdrawals: the big withdrawal in the year you took everything out, and the smaller ones in the years you were taking periodic

> payments. If you waited until you were 59½, you would be able to withdraw the entire balance of the IRA without penalty.

This rule raises an issue: what happens if you withdraw the entire balance of your traditional IRA in order to convert it to a Roth IRA? Will you pay a penalty in that case?

Fortunately, the answer is no. The regulations on Roth IRAs say that you can make the conversion without penalty—if you continue to receive the periodic distributions you were receiving before the conversion. The difference is that after the conversion you'll receive the payments from your Roth IRA. Remember, you'll have penalties going back to when you first began to receive periodic payments from your traditional IRA if you alter your payment schedule before satisfying the time requirement.

> Q: What about the rule that says I pay a 10% early distribution penalty if I withdraw from a Roth IRA within five years after a conversion?
>
> A: This rule is designed to prevent you from using a Roth IRA conversion to avoid the penalty for early distributions from traditional IRAs. It doesn't apply to distributions that qualify for exceptions to the penalty, so there's no penalty for 72t distributions.

Source of funds to pay tax on conversion. Generally it's advisable to pay conversion taxes from sources other than IRA funds. This is even more important when you're receiving periodic payments. You have to be certain that you don't have to use IRA funds (other than the periodic payment itself) to cover your tax liability on the conversion. If you have to take additional money from the IRA for this purpose, you'll violate the requirement to keep your periodic payments unchanged and end up paying penalties as described earlier.

Conversion following recharacterization

If you used the recharacterization rules to undo a previous conversion, you can't re-convert the same amount right away. You have to wait until you satisfy *both* of these conditions:

- The new conversion can't be in the same year as the old conversion.
- The new conversion has to be more than 30 days after the recharacterization you used to undo the old conversion.

See *Undoing and redoing a conversion* in Chapter 23.

Direct conversion of employer account

Originally we had little to say on the subject of converting 401k and other employer accounts: the only way to do this was to roll the employer account to a traditional IRA, and then convert the IRA. It's now possible to move directly from an employer account to a Roth IRA. In some situations this method produces results that aren't available when doing a two-step rollover and then conversion.

One requirement remains the same: you need to receive an *eligible rollover distribution.* Even though you're doing a direct conversion instead of a regular rollover, your payout has to be the kind that you would be allowed to roll to traditional IRA—for example, it can't be a hardship distribution or a minimum required distribution. Rollovers are discussed in Chapter 28.

Avoiding aggregation. One reason you might choose a direct rollover is to avoid the aggregation rule that applies to IRAs. If you have basis (after-tax money) in your employer account, and also have an existing IRA, a direct conversion may provide a better result than the two-step approach, as discussed in the next chapter.

Inherited employer account. You can't convert an inherited IRA. If you roll an inherited employer account to a traditional IRA, you have to treat it as an inherited IRA, so you can't convert it. However, the law appears to permit a direct transfer from an inherited traditional employer account to a Roth IRA. You have to treat the Roth as an inherited IRA, but you've accomplished the conversion.

Recharacterization. You can use the recharacterization rules to undo the tax consequences of a direct conversion from an employer plan to a Roth IRA, but the money doesn't go back to the employer plan. In this case the money will go to a traditional IRA, so that in the future it will be subject to IRA rules, not employer plan rules.

SIMPLE. If you participate in a SIMPLE plan, be aware that a special rule prohibits you from converting your account until you've satisfied a two-year participation requirement.

In-plan conversion

We now have yet another possible way to convert a 401k or similar account, called an *in-plan conversion.* The money goes from a traditional account to a Roth account within the same plan. This method allows you to continue to enjoy any benefits you receive from having money in the plan, such as investment opportunities or the ability to borrow against your account.

This method isn't available to all participants of all plans. Employers aren't required to offer Roth accounts in their retirement plans, and even if they offer Roth accounts they aren't required to offer in-plan conversions. What's more, employers who offer these conversions are permitted to impose restrictions, such as limiting the frequency of these conversions , or allowing them only when you're able to take an eligible rollover distribution.

> Initially the law permitted these conversions only when the account owner was able to take an eligible rollover distribution. This is no longer a legal requirement, but employers are permitted to impose this limitation and may do so if they feel it makes the plan less complicated. Such a restriction could prevent you from doing an in-plan Roth conversion even if your employer offers this alternative to plan participants meeting the requirements imposed by the plan.

If an in-plan conversion seems attractive, check to see if the plan offers this option, and whether you satisfy any requirements imposed by the plan.

Beneficiaries and alternate payees. The only beneficiary permitted to do an in-plan conversion after the death of the account owner is a surviving spouse. The only alternate payees who can do this are spouses and former spouses.

No recharacterization. In-plan conversions have one major disadvantage relative to other types of conversions: *they cannot be undone using a recharacterization.* Once you make an in-plan conversion you're stuck with it, even if you change your mind the next day. If your investments lose value, you'll still have to pay tax based on their value as of the date of the conversion.

Glitch fixed. An apparent drafting error in the law raised a question as to whether an in-plan conversion starts the five-year clock that determines when you'll be able to take a qualified distribution from your Roth account, leading us to recommend in an earlier edition of this book that you should make at least a small regular contribution to the Roth account that received this conversion, if possible. Subsequent guidance from the IRS makes it clear that an in-plan conversion does start the five-year clock (if it has not started earlier due to a designated Roth contribution), making this protective measure unnecessary.

Further details. Here are some other points the IRS addressed in guidance dealing with these conversions:

- If you convert an account at a time when you have a plan loan outstanding, the loan transfers to the Roth account and is treated as a continuation of the existing loan rather than a new loan.
- Spousal consent is not required for an in-plan conversion.
- If you have a right to receive a distribution from your account before the in-plan conversion, that right is preserved after the conversion.

22

Conversion Consequences

Generally you'll have to pay tax when converting a traditional retirement account to a Roth IRA.

CONVERTING A TRADITIONAL ACCOUNT TO A ROTH IRA can have highly favorable long-term consequences, for all the reasons discussed in Part II of this book. To secure those benefits, however, you have to pay whatever tax applies to the conversion. The basic rule here is simple: you pay the same tax you would have paid if you simply withdrew this money from your account, except the 10% early distribution penalty tax won't apply even if you're under 59½ at the time of the distribution. There are two main issues:

- What is the amount converted?
- How much of that amount is taxable?

This chapter covers these issues and related considerations.

Amount converted

The amount converted is the *value* of everything that was transferred from the traditional account to the Roth, determined as of the date of the transfer. A transfer of assets other than cash—stocks, bonds, mutual fund shares or other assets—requires a determination of the value of those items as of the date of the transfer. The original cost of those items doesn't matter.

Amount taxable

For most conversions, the amount taxable is the same as the amount converted. If you convert $50,000, you have to pay tax on $50,000. This assumes you have no *basis* in the account you're converting. If you're converting an IRA (instead of a 401k or other employer account) this also assumes you have no basis in any other traditional IRA.

Your basis is the cumulative amount of nondeductible contributions you've made over the years, reduced by any basis you recovered in connection with earlier distributions or conversions. The fraction of the overall value that represents basis determines the fraction of your conversion that is non-taxable.

> **Example:** You have only one traditional IRA with a total value of $10,000. You've made $4,000 in nondeductible contributions to the IRA, and the rest of the value represents deductible contributions or investment earnings. You convert $5,000 from this IRA to a Roth.

Your basis represents 40% of the total value, so $2,000 of the conversion (40% of $5,000) is nontaxable. You'll report $3,000 of income for this conversion.

If you have more than one traditional IRA, you're required to treat them as a single IRA in applying this rule. That's true even if they're completely separate IRAs, maintained at different financial institutions and containing money from different sources (for example, one you built up with annual contributions and another you created when you rolled over a 401k distribution). You have to include any IRA you have under an employer's SEP or SIMPLE plan as well.

> **Example:** You have two traditional IRAs, each worth $5,000. One has a basis of $4,000 (you made nondeductible contributions in that amount and the other $1,000 represents growth in your investments). You created the other IRA by rolling money from a traditional 401k account, and you never made any nondeductible contributions to that account.

If you convert one of these IRAs, you have to treat 60% of the conversion amount as taxable income. You get the same result no matter which IRA you convert (when you convert the same dollar amount), because the taxable amount is determined by treating all your traditional IRAs as a single IRA.

> Q: Do I get a different result if I convert one particular asset rather than another—for example, an asset that went down in value after I bought it in my traditional account?
>
> A: No. Converting an asset that's worth $4,000 is the same as converting $4,000 of cash, even if you originally bought that asset for a greater or smaller amount.

Although the amount converted is determined as of the date of the conversion, the calculation of the percentage taxable is based on the account value as of the end of the year, with certain adjustments. That percentage may change, for example, as a result of investment performance of the assets remaining in the traditional IRA, or as a result of a rollover from an employer plan to an IRA occurring after the conversion but within the same year. For details of the basis calculation see Form 8606 and instructions for that form.

Direct conversion of employer account

As explained in Chapter 21, conversion of an employer account no longer requires two separate steps. If you're eligible to roll money from a 401k (or 403b or 457) to a traditional IRA, you can move money directly from the employer plan to a Roth IRA.

Generally a direct conversion will have the same tax consequences as a two-step conversion. There's a potential difference, though, if you have an IRA as well as a 401k account, and one account has basis.

> **Example:** You have a traditional IRA with a value of $10,000 and no basis. Your 401k account also happens to be worth $10,000 but has basis of $4,000 because of nondeductible contributions. You're about to receive a full payout from the 401k plan.

If you convert the 401k account directly, you'll report $6,000 of taxable income—the same amount as if you simply withdrawn the money from the 401k without rolling it to another retirement account. In a two-step conversion, though, your 401k money would first go to an IRA. When you took the second step, converting the $10,000 rollover IRA, you would report $8,000 of income, because overall you have $20,000 in two IRAs and $4,000 of basis.

> If you're in the reverse situation, with basis in the IRA but not in the 401k account, the better choice (assuming you want to convert only $10,000) would be to convert the IRA instead of the 401k. Wait until the following year before receiving the 401k distribution and rolling it to a traditional IRA. That approach would allow you to recover the entire $4,000 of basis in the IRA.

Special tax rules not available. The IRS says that in a direct conversion you can't use rules that are available in some situations to reduce the tax on distributions from employer plans. Special provisions relating to net unrealized appreciation ("NUA") when a plan distributes stock of the company maintaining the plan don't apply if the stock is rolled to a Roth IRA. The same is true of optional methods for calculating tax for certain distributions to participants born on or before January 1, 1936. To use these rules you must receive a qualifying distribution that is *not* converted to a Roth IRA.

Recharacterizing a direct conversion. When you convert a traditional IRA to a Roth IRA and subsequently undo the conversion, the money goes back to a traditional IRA and you're in the same position as if you hadn't done the conversion in the first place. Things work a little differently if you have to recharacterize a direct conversion from a 401k account. The rules don't provide a way for you to send the money back to the 401k account, so instead you would send the money to a traditional IRA. The result is the same as if you did a tax-free rollover from the 401k to the IRA, but not necessarily the same as if the money remained in the 401k. In particular, if a direct conversion gave you a better result in terms of basis recovery as described above, you will have lost that opportunity, because any subsequent conversion will be from an IRA, using the basis recovery rules for those accounts.

> **Example:** The facts are the same as in the previous example, except you convert the 401k account with $4,000 of basis and later decide a conversion wasn't a good idea. You recharacterize the transfer, moving the money to a traditional IRA. If you try a $10,000 conversion again the next year, with the account value unchanged, you'll recover only $2,000 of basis because the conversion comes from an IRA, and your total basis for all IRAs is just 20% of their total value.

In-plan conversion

The tax consequences of an in-plan conversion (where money moves from a non-Roth account to a Roth account within the same employer plan) are generally the same as the consequences of a direct conversion from an employer plan account to a Roth IRA. As noted in Chapter 21, the recharacterization rules don't apply to in-plan conversions. This means there's no way to undo one of these conversions if you regret it later.

You may also want to be aware of the way distribution rules apply to Roth accounts in employer plans. These rules are not the same as the distribution rules for Roth IRAs. See Chapter 32.

Year taxable

It's possible to have a conversion that straddles two taxable years. In a trustee-to-trustee transfer, your old IRA provider may ship the money or assets to the new one so close to the end of the year that the new one doesn't set up the account until January. More commonly this might happen in a rollover-type conversion, where you take money from a traditional IRA and, within 60 days, put that money in a Roth IRA. In either of these cases the tax consequences of the conversion apply in the year of the distribution from the traditional account, not in the year the conversion was completed.

> To have a conversion in the later year, you have to wait until January to take the money or other assets out of the traditional account.

Although the conversion is taxable in the year of the distribution from the traditional account, we look to the year of contribution to determine when five years have elapsed from the conversion. This could make a difference in whether a later distribution is a qualified distribution, and it can also make a difference in whether a nonqualified distribution is subject to the 10% early distribution penalty if you take money from the IRA less than five years later. See Part VI for details on the tax treatment of distributions.

Ordinary income, not capital gain

The income you report on a conversion is based on the *value* of the account at the time of the conversion, not the original cost of the investments. An increase in value may be partly from growth in stocks or mutual funds that normally produce capital gain. In a retirement account that doesn't matter: any income you have from a conversion or distribution is ordinary income. It doesn't qualify for the lower rates that apply to long-term capital gain.

No early distribution penalty

Normally, if you take a taxable distribution from an IRA before age 59½ you pay a 10% early distribution penalty unless you can fit within one of the exceptions. An exception has been created for Roth conversions, so you won't pay a penalty on your conversion even if you're under age 59½.

> A special rule applies the 10% early distribution penalty to any withdrawal you take from converted amounts within five years after the conversion if you're under 59½ and not eligible for any of the exceptions.

Estimated tax

Most people don't have to pay estimated tax if most or all of their income is from compensation that's subject to withholding. But ordinarily there won't be any withholding on the income you report when you convert a traditional account to a Roth IRA. It's possible you'll have to pay a penalty if you don't make estimated tax payments to cover some or all of the tax you'll owe on a conversion.

Depending on your circumstances, you may be able to avoid penalties without making any estimated tax payments.

> **Example:** Last year you earned $60,000 and your withholding was enough to cover the full amount of your tax. In this year you earn $62,000 and you also convert a traditional IRA to a Roth IRA, reporting an additional $30,000 of income. Although you owe a substantial amount of tax on this additional income, you fall within an exception to the requirement to make estimated tax payments. The reason is that your withholding for this year is at least equal to the amount of tax you paid last year.

It's a good idea to become familiar with the rules for estimated payments if you report income from a Roth conversion. These rules are discussed in our free online Guide to Estimated Taxes at Fairmark.com.

Spreading conversion income

On two occasions—once when the Roth IRA was first introduced, and again in 2010 when the conversion rules were revised—we had special rules making it possible to spread the income from a conversion over multiple years. These rules have expired, so we no longer offer guidance on them.

23

Recharacterizing Conversions

The recharacterization rules allow you to undo a conversion retroactively.

IT'S THE SWISS ARMY KNIFE OF IRA TOOLS. We saw in Chapter 19 that you can use a recharacterization to switch an IRA contribution from one type of account to another retroactively. They're more commonly used as a way to undo a Roth conversion.

For the benefit of those who aren't reading straight through this book, we repeat in this chapter some of the rules concerning recharacterizations covered in Chapter 19.

Recharacterization

About the only unfriendly thing about this rule is the seven-syllable word used to describe it. A better description, in just three syllables: it's a do-over. This rule allows you to change something you did in the past, and treat it as if that's the way you did it in the first place. When you recharacterize a conversion, you're treated as if the money went into a traditional IRA (possibly the same one from which you took the money in the first place) instead of a Roth. If you follow all the rules, it's as if you traveled back in time: you get to pretend the conversion never happened.

Well, almost. Some lingering effects are described later under *Consequences of undoing a conversion.* Also, this rule doesn't allow you to recover fees you may have incurred in connection with the conversion. In fact, your IRA provider may charge a fee to cover the paperwork of the recharacterization. And a recharacterization doesn't undo the results of an unfortunate investment. This is an almost magical way to undo the *tax* consequences of an earlier action, but that's as far as it goes.

> The money or other assets you transfer in a recharacterization will be adjusted for investment performance as described later.

How it works

A recharacterization is similar to a conversion. You're moving money from one type of IRA to another. Unlike a conversion, though, you can't do a rollover-type of transfer, where you take money out of one IRA and, within 60 days, transfer it into another. That means you have just two possible ways to accomplish a recharacterization:

- Transfer the money or other assets from the Roth to a traditional IRA while keeping it at the same IRA provider.
- Move the money or other assets directly from your Roth IRA at provider to a traditional IRA at a different provider in a trustee-to-trustee transfer.

The first method is usually easier because it involves just one IRA provider. You'll fill out whatever form they provide, telling them what you want to do, and they'll take care of the rest. Even if you plan to move the money to a different IRA provider, it might be easier to do the recharacterization at the first one and then move the money in a rollover or trustee-to-trustee transfer. You can combine a recharacterization with a transfer to a different trustee if that approach happens to fit your situation, but it requires you to coordinate the actions of two IRA providers that may or may not play well together.

> In either case, follow up afterward to make certain the recharacterization took place as you intended. The IRS determines your tax consequences based on what the IRA provider actually did, not what you *told* them to do.

Q: If I'm using a recharacterization to undo a conversion, does the money have to go back to the original retirement account?

A: No, this money can go to an entirely different account. It can even be an account with a different IRA provider that wasn't involved in the conversion.

Possible uses

At one time recharacterizations were useful in recovering from failed conversions, where someone found out after the fact that they didn't qualify for a conversion. We don't have to worry about that problem now that the filing status and income limitations on conversions are gone. Yet recharacterizations continue to be tremendously useful in connection with conversions. You can undo a conversion if you find that you don't have enough money to cover the tax cost, or because your investments performed poorly after the conversion, or simply because you changed your mind about whether this would be a good strategy. You don't have to justify a recharacterization. If you want to undo a conversion, go ahead and undo it.

Q: I converted my 401k account. Can I undo that conversion?

A: If you converted it to a Roth IRA, you can recharacterize it by moving the money to a traditional IRA, but not back to the employer plan. If you converted it to a Roth account within the employer plan (an in-plan conversion), the tax law does not allow a recharacterization.

Q: What if I want to move just part of a conversion amount?

A: No problem. Recharacterization is not an all-or-nothing proposition. However, you have to move earnings related to whatever portion of the conversion you're moving.

Q: Can I specify which conversion is being recharacterized?

A: Yes. For example, if you did one conversion in January and another in June, you can undo the June conversion while leaving the January conversion in place, even if both went into the same Roth IRA. You might want to do this if you had strong investment performance between January and June, for example.

Q: Suppose I did a conversion, and afterward I did a rollover. Can I still do a recharacterization? Do I have to involve the IRA provider that handled the conversion?

A: Yes you can still do a recharacterization (assuming you're still inside the time limit), and no you don't have to involve the earlier trustee unless for some reason you want to use this transaction to transfer money or assets back to that trustee.

Q: Suppose I use these rules to undo a conversion, and later change my mind. Can I undo a recharacterization?

A: *No!* Once you've done a recharacterization you're stuck with that decision. If you used this rule to undo a conversion, you can do a new conversion after a waiting period described later in this chapter. But you can't reinstate the original conversion.

When to act

Generally you can undo a conversion until October 15 of the year in which you file your tax return for the year to which the conversion relates. A conversion relates to the year in which the money came out of the traditional account, even if it didn't go into the Roth account until after the end of that year.

Qualifying for the October 15 deadline. Strictly speaking, the deadline for recharacterizations is the due date of your return, with extensions. Filing for an extension (Form 4868) extends your tax return due date to October 15, and also extends the recharacterization deadline to that date.

But there's also a special procedure that allows you to extend the recharacterization deadline to October 15 even if you filed your return by April 15 without getting an extension. To take advantage, you need to complete the recharacterization by October 15 and file an amended return (Form 1040-X) reflecting any changes required by the recharacterization, including, if necessary, a new or amended Form 8606. Write "Filed pursuant to section 301.9100-2" at the top of the amended return and file it where you filed the original return.

> This procedure is available only if you filed your original return by the April 15 deadline. If you slipped up, missing that deadline without filing for an extension, you won't qualify for the six-month extension, and you'll be stuck with an April 15 recharacterization deadline.

Leave plenty of time. It isn't enough for you to take action within this time limit. Your trustee has to complete the transfer before the deadline. It's best to take action well in advance so there's time to follow up and confirm that the trustee finished the paperwork.

Super-extended deadline

What if you discover a problem after the extended deadline has passed? Through the private letter ruling process, the IRS has granted an even longer extension to some taxpayers. They won't do this simply because you changed your mind about the conversion, or because your Roth IRA suffered investment losses. You'll probably have to show that the transaction you're trying to undo never would have happened in the first place except for an honest mistake, and that you took steps to correct the problem promptly after it was discovered.

This is your choice of last resort for undoing a bad conversion. For one thing, the IRS isn't required to grant your request. It helps to have the request handled by a tax professional with experience in this area, but even then success is not assured. In any event the process is expensive and time-consuming. Expect to pay the IRS a hefty filing fee in addition to any professional fees, and plan on the entire process taking months to complete.

It appears to me the IRS has been quite even-handed in responding to these requests, providing relief when there was an innocent mistake and the taxpayer took action promptly after the mistake was discovered.

Adjusting for investment performance

When you undo a conversion, the amount you transfer from the Roth to a traditional IRA has to be adjusted for investment performance during the time it was in the Roth. If the Roth increased in value, you have to increase the amount of the transfer. A decline in the value of the Roth would mean you transfer a smaller amount.

It doesn't matter whether the change in the account value represents income (such as dividends or interest) or simply a change in the value of assets, such as stock or mutual fund shares. The only thing that matters is the value of the account.

Moving part of an account. A recharacterization doesn't have to involve the entire balance of an account. Perhaps you're recharacterizing a conversion that put money into an existing Roth that held other assets. Or perhaps you're only recharacterizing part of a conversion, having decided the amount converted was too large.

In either case you'll have to adjust the amount you're moving to reflect the investment performance of the IRA during the period the money was in the account. The adjustment will be based on the overall performance of the IRA during this period, not the specific assets that were involved in the conversion you're recharacterizing. Because of this rule you may wish to consider segregating conversion assets, a strategy discussed in Chapter 25.

The earnings calculation. A tax regulation issued in 2003 lays out the details of the earnings calculation. The basic idea is simple: the amount you're switching will be adjusted by a percentage that represents the percentage change in the IRA that relates to investment performance during the period the money was in the account. The actual calculations can get complicated in some situations, though, so generally you should tell your IRA provider the unadjusted amount you want to move and let them figure out the earnings adjustment.

Consequences of undoing a conversion

When you recharacterize a conversion, your income tax is the same as if the conversion never occurred. Yet it isn't quite accurate to say that all consequences of the conversion have been erased:

- If you recharacterized only part of the conversion, you still have tax consequences from the part you left in place. You have to file Form 8606 and attach an explanation as described in the instructions for that form.
- If you recharacterized the entire conversion, you don't have to file Form 8606 but you still have to attach an explanation as described in the instructions for that form.
- As explained later in this chapter, after you undo a conversion there is a required waiting period before you can do a new one.
- If you used a rollover-type conversion (taking money out of the traditional account and then, within 60 days, putting it in the Roth), it appears that undoing the conversion will turn this transaction into a regular

rollover, subject to the rule that allows only one rollover per 12-month period.

Transfer before recharacterization

What if you transferred money from one IRA to another before making the recharacterization switch? For example:

- You converted a traditional IRA (IRA1) to a Roth IRA (IRA2).
- Then you rolled that Roth IRA (IRA2) to a different Roth IRA (IRA3) maintained by a different provider.
- Now you want to undo the original conversion with a transfer to a newly formed traditional IRA (IRA4).

That could be an awkward situation, because you're trying to recharacterize a conversion to an IRA that no longer exists. Fortunately the folks at Treasury foresaw this possibility when they wrote the regulations. These rules say you should disregard any tax-free transfers that occur between the date of the original conversion and the date you undo it.

> The trustee of IRA2 isn't involved at this point, but you should notify that trustee of the recharacterization anyway, because that trustee received the conversion you are now reversing.

Undoing and redoing a conversion

There are situations where you may want to undo a conversion so you can *redo* it with a better tax result. For example, you might convert in one year only to realize you'll be in a lower tax bracket the following year. More commonly, a conversion can produce unfavorable tax consequences if your investments lose value shortly thereafter. The amount of income you report is based on the value on the date of the conversion, not the value when you file your tax return and pay the tax.

> **Example:** You convert a $30,000 IRA that has no basis, and by the time you file your tax return the investments have lost a third of their value.

The investment loss is bad enough, but it adds insult to injury when you realize you have to pay tax on the full $30,000. If events happened the other way around—you had the investment loss in the traditional account and then did the conversion—you would be paying tax on just $20,000, the amount remaining after the investment loss.

Fortunately, in many cases it's possible to avoid the bad tax result. You can use a recharacterization to undo the conversion and, subject to limitations described below, do another conversion. There is absolutely nothing illegitimate about this sequence of transactions. Congress understood that this would be one possible use of the recharacterization rules when it wrote the law for Roth IRAs. Here are the main considerations.

Is it worth it? You should consider this strategy only if the losses following conversion are large enough, both as a percentage and in absolute dollars, to make it worthwhile. Fluctuation in value is a fact of life for many investments. Consider the costs in paperwork, including the value of your own time and the added complexity on your income tax return.

> If you undo a conversion after a small loss in value, the investment may recover before you have a chance to do a new conversion, defeating your goal to reconvert at a lower value.

Waiting period. If you undo a conversion, there's a required waiting period before you can do a new conversion of the same amount. You can do a new conversion right away if you're converting *different money* (see below), but when converting the same money you have to satisfy *both* of the following conditions:

- The new conversion can't be in the same year as the original conversion, *and*
- The new conversion can't be within the 30-day period beginning on the date you completed the recharacterization.

For purposes of the second requirement, the recharacterization is completed when the money is back in a traditional IRA. Check to see what the IRA provider's records indicate for this date before proceeding with a new conversion.

Don't jump too soon. Unless you can get around the waiting period by converting different money, as described next, it generally doesn't make sense to undo a conversion before December of the year it took place. That's because of the way the waiting period rule described above works.

> **Example:** You converted in January, and six months later the investments are down 20%. If you undo the conversion now, you'll have to wait until next January to redo it. If you undo it early in December, you can still redo it in early January (31 days after the recharacterization). There's no added benefit in undoing the conversion earlier, and delaying that action will allow you to see if your investments recover their losses in the meantime.

Converting different money. If you converted your entire IRA, you'll have to wait the required period after a recharacterization before doing a new conversion. If you converted only a portion, however, you can avoid the waiting period by converting a different portion.

> **Example:** You have a traditional IRA with a value of $100,000, and you decide to convert $30,000 of that amount to a Roth. Investments in the Roth perform poorly, and a few months later the account is worth only $20,000. If you leave the conversion in place, you'll have to pay tax on $30,000 despite having only $20,000 in the Roth. Instead, you can do a new conversion of $30,000, making sure the money goes to a separate Roth IRA. Then undo the first conversion, moving the remaining $20,000 back to a traditional IRA.

You haven't violated the waiting period, and you've restored the dollar amount you intended for your Roth without paying additional tax.

24

Conversion Strategy Fundamentals

Careful planning for conversions can produce better results.

THIS CHAPTER DISCUSSES THE MAIN PRINCIPLES to apply in planning a Roth conversion.

When in doubt, convert

You might have some uncertainty as to whether a conversion will be advantageous. My recommendation in these cases: if it seems reasonably likely that your conversion will work out, go ahead and do it. Don't allow uncertainty to stand in the way of a move that may enhance your retirement wealth.

That's because you can undo a conversion any time until October 15 of the following year, using the recharacterization rules. You may have some transaction costs related to the paperwork, but you can eliminate the tax consequences, treating the transaction as if it never occurred. On the other hand, if you *don't* convert, you're stuck with that decision. You may be able to convert later, but you can't go back in time to seize an advantage you would have had from an earlier conversion.

> Proceeding with a conversion preserves your choices until October 15 of the following year; failure to convert closes the door as of December 31 of the current year.

Your tax bracket

When planning a conversion you should determine the tax bracket in which it will be taxed. The conversion income might push you into a higher tax bracket, so that the tax cost of the conversion is higher than you might expect. In this situation it may make sense to convert only a portion of your account in the current year.

As we saw in Chapter 8, your tax bracket is *not* the rate your employer uses to determine the amount withheld from your paycheck. Withholding rates are aimed at the *average* rate of tax you're likely to pay on your income, after taking into account deductions and other tax benefits, so the total amount withheld will usually be roughly equal to the amount of tax you owe for the year. We're interested in knowing the *additional* amount of tax you'll pay on the *additional* amount of income you'll have as a result of the conversion.

To find that amount, we need to know your *taxable income.* This is not the same as the amount you earn. Taxable income is the amount that's left after you claim all your deductions, including such common items as the standard deduction and the deduction for personal exemptions. As a general rule, your taxable income is quite a bit lower than the amount you earn.

There's a line on your tax return (Form 1040, 1040A or 1040EZ) for taxable income. Be sure you're looking at *taxable* income, not total income or adjusted gross income.

Unless you're already in the highest tax bracket, the rate you pay on additional income will increase when your taxable income goes over the amount set for that tax rate. Those levels depend on your filing status, and they're adjusted each year for inflation. The most important breakpoint is between the 15% and 25% brackets. The ten-percentage-point gap between these two brackets is the largest single jump in rates.

The benefits of a Roth conversion can overcome the cost of an unfavorable rate shift in the other brackets. It might make sense to pay 33% tax on a conversion when projections indicate the money will eventually be withdrawn at a tax rate of 28%. The larger effective size of the Roth and the ability to avoid required minimum distributions can outweigh the tax rate differential.

If you project a 25% or higher rate on the conversion and a 15% rate in retirement, however, the conversion strategy may be unwise. A 25% tax is 67% higher than a 15% tax. The benefits of a Roth conversion can recover against a smaller tax rate differential, but spreadsheet models indicate this mountain is likely to be too steep to climb.

For 2015, the level of taxable income where you switch from the 15% bracket to the 25% bracket is $37,450 for singles, $50,200 for heads of households, and $74,900 when married filing jointly. Current numbers are available in the Reference Room of our website at Fairmark.com.

Converting in installments

You may find that you can convert only a portion of your IRA within your current tax bracket. In this situation a partial conversion could be the best strategy. The following year you may be able to convert an additional increment within that bracket. The total tax you pay when spreading the conversion over a period of two or more years can be smaller than the cost of converting everything in a single year.

You may have other reasons for dividing your conversion among two or more years:

- It may be easier to come up with the money to pay tax on the conversion income if you convert in installments.
- If you have to undo a conversion, you have a waiting period before you can do a new conversion of the same amount, but if you did a partial conversion you can do a new conversion of *different money* without waiting as explained in Chapter 23.

You should be aware of a possible drawback to this approach. If the value remaining in the traditional IRA increases before you can complete the conversion in the later year, you'll be paying tax on a greater amount of income. You may end up paying a greater overall amount of tax even though the rate of tax is lower.

> **Example:** You convert half your $20,000 IRA in one year and wait to convert the other half. In the meantime your investments perform brilliantly, causing the unconverted part to grow to a value of $14,000.

Even if you're paying tax at a lower rate, you now have to pay tax on $14,000 instead of $10,000. Depending on the size of the difference in tax rates, you may end up paying more tax to complete your conversion than if you simply went ahead with the entire $20,000 conversion in the first year.

Timing your conversion

The amount of tax you pay on a conversion is based on the *value* of the assets transferred. That means the timing of your conversion can have a big impact on the amount converted, especially if your account is invested in stocks or other assets that can change in value rapidly. The result is favorable if you convert when the account is at a relatively low value and see it rise in value afterward, because you paid a relatively small amount of conversion tax to end up with an account of that size. The reverse situation, converting when stock prices are high and seeing the account lose value, is undesirable.

For this reason, it may seem logical to convert your IRA ahead of an expected increase in stock market values, or delay a conversion when the market appears likely to fall. Unfortunately, while many experts offer predictions of short-term stock market movements, often backed by cogent arguments, their predictions are entirely unreliable. In fact, there are *always* experts predicting that the market is about to collapse, and others predicting it's about to take off toward new highs. There is simply no way to know how the stock market is going to perform over any given period of time. Timing your conversion based on these predictions is not a sound strategy.

Time of year. There's another kind of timing that may be helpful, though. As a general rule it's better to do a conversion earlier in the year, for two reasons.

One has to do with the due date for paying tax on the conversion income. If you convert in January you won't have to pay that tax until about fifteen months later. Your Roth can be generating tax-free earnings more than a year before you have to come up with the conversion tax. You'll pay tax on a December conversion only about four months after the transaction. The difference won't be quite this great if you have to make estimated payments covering tax on the conversion income, but even then some of the advantage of an earlier conversion usually remains. This advantage applies whether you're converting to a Roth IRA or doing an in-plan conversion of a traditional 401k or similar account to a Roth account within the plan.

The other advantage from converting early in the year comes from the opportunity to undo a conversion if your investments perform poorly afterward. Your deadline for this choice is October 15 of the year after the conversion. That means you get as many as twenty-one months of hindsight for a conversion in January, but only about ten months for a conversion in December. This advantage applies only when converting to a Roth IRA, because the recharacterization rules allow you to undo these conversions. You aren't allowed to undo an in-plan Roth conversion.

There's one factor that points the other way. Converting late in the year, rather than waiting until next year, may allow you to satisfy the five-year period for qualifying distributions, or the five-year period for avoiding a 10% early distribution penalty, a year earlier. That's because these five-year periods are measured from January 1 of the year the relevant event occurs. These considerations aren't always relevant, however, and you can start the clock running for qualified distributions with a small conversion before year-end and then convert the rest early in the following year.

Undoing and redoing a conversion

There are situations where it may make sense to undo a conversion so you can redo it at a lower tax cost. You might find yourself in a lower tax bracket the year after you did a conversion, for example. Another possibility: your investments may lose value after the conversion, so that you would report a smaller amount of income if you could erase the original conversion transaction and do a new one at the lower value. See Chapter 23 for an explanation of how to do this.

Paying the conversion tax

Most people who do a Roth conversion have to pay at least some tax as a result. Here are some tips on planning for payment of that tax.

Estimating the tax. It's rarely a good idea to move forward with a conversion without having a pretty good idea how much tax you'll pay. Usually the easiest way to get a reasonably close estimate is to pull out the previous year's tax return and figure out how much higher the tax would be if the conversion income is added to taxable income. For example, if the conversion income is $15,000 in the current year, add $15,000 to your taxable income for the previous year. Then look up the new taxable income amount in the tax tables to see how much higher the tax is. Of course this method isn't accurate if your filing status has changed or if your income or deductions are significantly different in the current year.

This simplified method doesn't take into account various ways the conversion income might affect your tax return, though. For example, this added income might cause you to lose part of a credit you claim for dependent care or college tuition for your children. To get a more accurate estimate of the actual tax cost of the conversion, a tax pro might take your prior year return and redo it, plugging in not only the added income from the conversion but also estimated adjustments for other significant changes. Normally it isn't necessary to go through all the same detailed work you would do in preparing an actual return, but it can be helpful to work through the return, rather than just tack a number onto your taxable income. That way, unpleasant surprises are less likely.

If you used software to prepare your return last year, you may be able to get a pretty accurate estimate fairly easily. Just fire up the software and plug in additional income representing the conversion and any other changes you expect for this year. Using tax software often makes it much easier to play "what-if."

> I usually don't worry about the inflation adjustments for tax brackets from one year to the next in doing this kind of estimate. Those changes are seldom significant for this purpose, and they can provide a helpful margin of error.

Early distribution penalty. You may find that it's difficult to come up with money to pay the conversion tax without tapping your retirement account. If you're under 59½, the result may be a 10% penalty. There are a number of exceptions to this early distribution penalty, but none that applies specifically to your need to pay tax on a Roth conversion.

It's possible for the advantages of a conversion to outweigh the disadvantages even when you pay this penalty. For example, you may have unusual circumstances allowing you to convert in a tax year when your tax rate is much lower than normal. Another possibility is a situation where your basis in the account represents a large fraction of the overall value, as discussed next.

Account has basis. Using part of the retirement account to pay the tax may not be as bad, even when paying the 10% early distribution penalty, if you have enough basis in the account from nondeductible contributions. The penalty applies only to the part of the distribution that's taxable, and the part of a distribution representing a return of basis is nontaxable.

There's a key point to keep in mind if you plan to handle the tax payment this way. *You should take the tax money from the traditional account before the conversion, not from the Roth after the conversion.* When you take a distribution from a traditional IRA, you recover a portion of your basis determined as described in the Chapter 22 under the heading *Amount taxable.* If basis represents 75% of the value of the account, you can withdraw money and pay tax on only 25% of the distribution. The 10% penalty will apply to the same portion that's taxable.

This rule doesn't apply if you take money from the Roth account after the conversion. The first dollars you take out will come from any regular contributions you made to that account, and that's good, because those distributions are free of tax or penalty. But after that, the next dollars come from the *taxable* portion of the conversion money. There's no added tax on this distribution because you're already paying tax on the conversion, but the penalty will apply to the entire distribution, up to the amount that was taxable.

> **Example:** You have a traditional IRA and, up to now, you do not have a Roth. Your traditional IRA has a value of $25,000 and $20,000 of basis, so you'll pay tax on only $5,000 when you convert the entire amount. You plan to use $2,000 of that amount to cover federal and state income tax on the conversion income.

If you withdraw the $2,000 from the Roth after the conversion you'll be treated as taking the entire amount from the taxable portion of the conversion, so you'll be hit with a $200 penalty on top of the tax on $5,000. Instead, you can take the $2,000 from the traditional IRA, setting it aside to pay tax and converting the rest. You still pay income tax on $5,000, but you reduced your penalty to $40 because it applies only to the taxable part of the distribution ($400 out of the $2,000).

Size of the account. There's another reason to avoid tapping the retirement account for the tax payment, if possible. One of the key advantages of the Roth IRA arises because it's effectively larger than a traditional IRA. As explained in Chapter 6, a traditional account works partly for the benefit of the Treasury, because the more it grows, the more tax the IRS will collect on the distributions. In a Roth account, all the money is working for you, so a Roth of the same apparent size is effectively bigger.

You give up this advantage, or at least some of it, if you use money from the retirement account to pay tax on the conversion. In effect, you're making the account smaller at the same time you're making it bigger. You may still achieve other advantages from the conversion, but you're leaving a big one on the table.

> Despite these observations, taxpayers over 59½ can still gain significant advantages from a conversion even if they use part of the account to pay the tax. Other benefits include avoiding the minimum distribution requirement that applies to traditional accounts and preventing subsequent retirement account distributions from increasing the amount of tax paid on social security benefits.

Safe and secure. Regardless of whether you're tapping your retirement account to pay the tax, you should make sure the money you need for this purpose is safe and secure. Be sure to set this money aside, and resist any temptation to make speculative investments with this part of your assets. Content yourself with whatever you can earn in a money market fund or perhaps a certificate of deposit that matures before the tax falls due.

25

Advanced Conversion Strategies

Here are some additional ways to get better results from a Roth conversion.

WE TURN NOW TO SPECIAL TECHNIQUES that can enhance the benefits of a Roth conversion.

Net investment income tax

Since 2013 higher-income taxpayers have paid a 3.8% surtax on investment income, including interest, dividends and capital gains. You can be hit with this tax when your adjusted gross income (modified to add back foreign earned income, if you took advantage of that exclusion) exceeds:

- $250,000 if you're married filing jointly or a surviving widow or widower;

- $200,000 if you're single or a head of household;
- $125,000 if you're married filing separately.

These threshold amounts are not adjusted for inflation.

> **Example:** If you're single with AGI of $205,000, including $25,000 of net investment income, you pay this tax on $5,000, because that's how much is above the $200,000 threshold. If your AGI is $240,000, the entire $25,000 of net investment income is taxed.

Income from retirement plan distributions, including Roth conversions (which are taxed like distributions) is not subject to the tax. Yet conversion income counts as part of your overall income in determining whether you're one of those higher-income taxpayers who have to pay this tax on their net investment income.

> **Example:** Before taking retirement income into account, your adjusted gross income, including $20,000 in net investment income, is $10,000 below the threshold amount. A $40,000 Roth conversion would not be included in net investment income but it would push your AGI above the threshold amount so that you now pay net investment income tax on the $20,000 of investment income that otherwise would have escaped the tax.

In this example, the conversion results in paying more net investment income tax, which may count as a factor against converting, or a reason to change conversion plans, so that some or all of it occurs in a different year. In other situations a conversion may produce savings in net investment income tax, as it would reduce or eliminate the need to take taxable retirement plan distributions in years following the year of the conversion.

Roth conversion planning for individuals who have substantial income from investments outside their retirement accounts should take the net investment income tax into account.

Segregating conversion assets

If you already have a Roth IRA, you don't have to create a new one to do a conversion. You can move money from a traditional IRA into an existing Roth, if you want. Starting a new Roth for your conversion involves added paperwork, and may result in added fees from your IRA provider.

There's a possible advantage in keeping the conversion assets in a separate IRA, though, at least initially. You might do this if you want the flexibility to undo the conversion later based on the performance of the investments made with the conversion money.

> **Example:** You have a Roth IRA worth $60,000 and a traditional IRA worth $20,000. Early in the year, you convert the traditional IRA, moving the $20,000 to the existing Roth, and using this money to make a speculative investment. A year later you find that the new investment has done poorly—in fact, it lost half its value. At the same time, your other investments in the Roth have done well, rising in value by $10,000, so overall your IRA broke even on its investments for this period.

At this point it would be nice if you could move the new investment, now worth $10,000, back to a traditional IRA. The idea would be to eliminate $20,000 of conversion income from your tax return and, after the required waiting period, convert again at the lower value, with a significantly smaller tax cost. Unfortunately you can't do that because the earnings calculation looks at the IRA as a whole. You aren't allowed to trace the results to particular assets. You can undo the $20,000 conversion, but you would have to move $20,000 back to the traditional IRA because overall there is no earnings adjustment. You would not be able to convert again later at a lower cost.

You would be in a much better situation if you had kept the conversion money in a separate Roth IRA. Although there are some situations where you have to treat all your Roth IRAs as a single IRA, this is not one of them. The regulations specifically state that if the conversion money is in a separate IRA you can undo the entire conversion by transferring the entire contents of that IRA back to a traditional IRA. In this example you would eliminate $20,000 of conversion income from your tax return while moving only $10,000 from the Roth, and later you would have the opportunity to convert at a lower cost.

> Once the deadline for undoing the conversion has passed, you can use a rollover to combine the two Roth IRAs.

Unfortunately, we've seen people have difficulty in using this approach. The trustee may not understand you want a separate Roth IRA for this purpose, or may not cooperate in using the rule that calls for a separate earnings calculation for a separate Roth IRA. If you have an existing Roth IRA and plan to create another one with the same trustee, hash this out with them ahead of time, and if possible get something from them in writing acknowledging that this is your intent.

Multiple IRAs for a single conversion. Some people take this idea a step further, dividing a single conversion into multiple conversions with money going into separate Roth IRAs for each type of investment. For example, instead of a single $60,000 conversion, you might convert $20,000 to a Roth that will invest in small cap stocks, another $20,000 to a Roth that will invest in emerging markets, and yet another $20,000 into a Roth that will hold a commodity fund. Later, you can undo one or more of these conversions separately depending on the performance of those investments.

> Judge for yourself whether the probability of a worthwhile payoff is great enough to justify the paperwork and any other costs.

Opposing investments. Another version of this strategy tries to gain a tax advantage from making investments that are designed to move in opposite directions. For example, you could convert half into a Roth that will invest in a fund that goes up when the S&P 500 goes up, and the other half in a fund that is intentionally designed to go up when the S&P 500 goes *down*. The idea is that no matter which way the stock index moves, one fund will go up and the other will go down, and you can undo the conversion went down while keeping the other one.

My opinion: this is too clever by half. You're adopting a lousy investment strategy in hopes of getting a tax payoff that may not materialize. I describe the strategy here for the sake of completeness, but I would never recommend it.

Isolating IRA basis

If your traditional IRA holds both pre-tax and after-tax money, you have to treat any distribution from that account, including a conversion, as coming from both categories proportionately. Because of the aggregation rule, the same is true if you have pre-tax money in one traditional IRA and after-tax money in another.

> **Example:** Your traditional IRA is worth $25,000, and you've made $5,000 in after-tax contributions. If you convert $5,000 to a Roth, you can't treat the entire amount as coming from after-tax dollars. Instead, you'll have to

> treat $4,000 as taxable income, because 80% of the IRA is pre-tax money. The same would be true if you held the after-tax money in a separate traditional IRA and you converted only that IRA, because you have to treat all traditional IRAs as a single IRA in figuring the tax consequences of a conversion.

These rules can stand in the way of a backdoor Roth IRA contribution strategy (Chapter 16) or simply prevent you from extracting the after-tax money from your traditional IRA for a tax-free Roth conversion. There is a possible solution, however.

Employer plans are now permitted to accept rollovers from traditional IRAs, provided that the amount rolled over doesn't exceed the amount that would be taxable if you withdrew all the money from the IRA. You have to report this rollover on your tax return, but you don't pay tax on any income until you take withdrawals from the employer plan. When you roll all the taxable money from the traditional IRA to an employer plan, the amount remaining in the traditional IRA is equal to its basis. That means you can convert the traditional IRA to a Roth without reporting any income.

There are a number of considerations in using this approach. You have to keep in mind that all your traditional IRAs are treated as a single IRA for purposes of determining the taxable and nontaxable portion. That means you can't use this approach to eliminate the taxable portion of one traditional IRA while retaining another traditional IRA that holds taxable money.

You also have to keep in mind that this rollover has other consequences. The investment opportunities in the employer plan may or may not be as good as the ones you had available in your IRA. What's more, you may not be able to demand a distribution from an employer plan whenever you want, the way you can with an IRA.

Perhaps the most important problem in using this strategy is that although the law permits employers to accept this kind of rollover, it doesn't *require* them to do so. Many employers feel these rollovers pose potential problems for their retirement plans and refuse to accept them.

Some people have solved this problem by setting up their own 401k plans. You can't do this if your only source of income is wages from your employer. If you have your own business, though, you may wish to consider whether this opportunity is valuable enough to justify the expenses of establishing and maintaining your own 401k plan.

> Many investment firms now offer a way to start "solo 401k" plans. Be sure to choose one that is designed to accept rollovers from IRAs.

One more point. It's likely that Congress intended to permit you to roll the pre-tax dollars to a 401k while leaving the after-tax dollars behind in the IRA. It appears that most tax pros interpret the law this way, and we've seen no indication that the IRS disagrees.

Yet there's some language in the law that might suggest a different interpretation. It seems to say we have to divide the *distribution* between pre-tax and after-tax dollars, and then roll only the pre-tax dollars to a 401k. If that's the rule, then in our earlier example it wouldn't work if you simply take $20,000 out of the IRA and roll it to a 401k, because 20% of the distribution would be treated as after-tax money.

> While it doesn't appear likely that the IRS will challenge these transactions, the safer approach (if available) would be to withdraw the entire $25,000 balance of the IRA, roll $20,000 to a 401k, and then roll (convert) the remaining $5,000 to a Roth IRA.

Isolating 401k basis

A similar issue arises when you have after-tax money in an employer plan account. Conversion of the entire account may be a good move, but some people want to convert only the after-tax dollars. We'll look first at what income might be included and then at how to isolate it.

No aggregation. When you figure the tax consequences of a distribution or conversion from an IRA, you have to aggregate all IRAs of the same kind (traditional or Roth). This aggregation rule doesn't apply to employer accounts. If you have a 401k with your current employer and another account in a 401k where you worked previously, the tax rules apply to each one separately.

In fact, you may not have to aggregate all the pre-tax and after-tax dollars in your account at a single employer. After-tax dollars accumulated before 1987 can be distributed with no allocation of pre-tax dollars. The proportionate distribution rule applies to non-Roth after-tax dollars accumulated later, but employers are permitted to maintain these amounts in a separate subaccount. The only pre-tax dollars in that subaccount are the investment earnings produced by the after-tax dollars. If your employer's plan has been set up this way, and you're able to withdraw money specifically from this subaccount, you'll receive a proportionate mix of the after-tax and pre-tax dollars *in that subaccount.* Other pre-tax dollars (your pre-tax contributions, employer match and investment earnings on those amounts) won't enter into the calculation.

Example: Overall you have $100,000 in your 401k account, including $9,000 in after-tax contributions made after 1986 and $1,000 of investment earnings on that portion of your account. If you're permitted to withdraw $10,000 from this portion of your account (your after-tax contributions and the earnings on that portion), you can remove all your after-tax dollars while leaving $90,000 in pre-tax dollars in the 401k.

This is permitted because of a rule in section 72(d)(2) of the Internal Revenue Code saying this portion of your account can be treated separately for purposes of the income allocation rules.

If you have only a modest amount of investment earnings on your after-tax contributions, as in the example above, you may not feel the need to isolate your contributions from the earnings. If you're willing to pay tax on the pre-tax dollars, only $1,000 in this case, you can simply move the entire $10,000 to a Roth. Yet we'll see next that it's easy now to isolate the after-tax dollars from the earnings, sending the pre-tax dollars to a traditional IRA in a tax-free rollover and at the same time sending the after-tax dollars to a Roth for a tax-free conversion.

This used to be hard. Prior to September 2014, anyone wanting to isolate the portion of a 401k distribution representing basis, for the purpose of a tax-free Roth conversion, had to grapple with some difficult rules. It appeared that the only safe way to do this was an awkward three-step process that required a single distribution paid out to the account owner, followed by two separate rollover contributions. This technique didn't work for a direct transfer from the 401k to the IRAs, and that meant the employer had to withhold income tax on the pre-tax portion of the payout. In many cases, the withholding requirement stood as an obstacle to completing the rollovers that were essential to the plan.

Now it's easy. In September 2014 the IRS announced a change in these rules. You still can't take a distribution that consists only of after-tax dollars (except the pre-1987 amounts mentioned above), but when you take a distribution that includes both pre-tax and after-tax dollars, you can have the pre-tax dollars go to a traditional IRA in a direct transfer (avoiding withholding) and send the after-tax dollars to a Roth. The entire transaction is tax-free: a rollover of pre-tax dollars to a traditional account, and a Roth conversion that consists only of after-tax dollars.

An important detail. Conceptually, this technique works only if the transfer to the traditional account and the transfer to the Roth are treated as two parts of a single transfer. If they're treated as two distinct payouts from the 401k plan, then each one will include proportionate amounts of pre-tax and after-tax dollars, defeating your intention to isolate basis. The IRS says you will get the desired treatment if the payments are "scheduled to be made at the same time (disregarding differences due to reasonable delays to facilitate plan administration)." It should be easy to satisfy this requirement, provided that you avoid the mistake of trying to take one category (pre-tax or after-tax) first and take the other later. Your goal is to do them both at once.

Part V
Managing Your Account

26 Tax Rules for IRA Investments

27 Investing Your Retirement Account

28 Rollovers and Direct Transfers

26

Tax Rules for IRA Investments

There are some special rules that apply to investments in an IRA.

YOU SHOULDN'T HAVE TO WORRY about special investment rules for your 401k account. The administrator should make sure the plan follows all the rules. It's a different story for IRAs. Normal investing won't get you in trouble, but you should be aware of certain rules, especially if you start getting creative.

Income, gains and losses in the account

For most purposes, your Roth account acts like a world where taxes don't exist. Your account can receive interest income, dividends, mutual fund distributions and capital gains without paying any tax. By the same token, you get no tax benefit from expenses and losses incurred within the account. That's just the flip side of the same coin: if you pay no tax on the income, you get no deduction for the losses.

Unrelated business taxable income. As always in the world of taxation, there's an exception. Certain types of investments produce *unrelated business taxable income* (UBTI). This income is taxable even when it's received by a qualified retirement account such as an IRA. You're wasting the tax benefit of your IRA if you use the funds there to make one of these investments. What's more, you may incur added fees from the trustee of your IRA if you make investments that require them to file forms relating to this tax.

Generally you don't have to worry about this issue if you stick with normal investments like stock, bonds, mutual funds and money market funds. If you're offered something out of the ordinary, such as partnership interests, watch out. Read the prospectus carefully to determine whether the investment produces UBTI.

> Your IRA can receive up to $1,000 UBTI per year before the tax applies.

Deducting a loss. If the investments in your Roth IRA perform poorly enough to produce an overall loss, there's a way to claim a deduction for that loss—but only if you take all the money from all your Roth IRAs. There are drawbacks to this approach, and important limitations. See Chapter 33 for details.

Investment expenses

Investors encounter expenses of various kinds. If the fees relate to an IRA, the question arises whether the fees should be paid by the owner of the IRA, with money held outside the IRA, or instead paid from money that's in the IRA. You may gain an advantage if you use money outside the IRA, because this approach enhances the size of your tax-favored retirement account. You may even gain an additional advantage by being able to claim an itemized deduction for the expense on your income tax return.

Trustee fees. Many IRA providers charge an annual fee for administrative expenses associated with maintaining an IRA account. If these fees are billed separately by the trustee, the IRS says you can pay them with money from outside the IRA. This payment will not be treated as a contribution to the IRA, even though it prevents a reduction in the size of the account. Normally these fees will qualify as miscellaneous itemized deductions. That means you may receive a tax benefit from paying them, but only if you itemize, and only if your miscellaneous deductions add up to more than 2% of your adjusted gross income.

> You can't claim a deduction if the fee is paid directly from the IRA, but if you're in a position to take money from a Roth IRA without paying tax or penalty you can achieve the desired result by taking a withdrawal, depositing it in your checking account, and then writing a check to cover the fee.

Brokerage commissions. A different rule applies to brokerage commissions. These are treated as part of the cost of buying and selling the relevant investments. If you use money from outside the IRA to pay these amounts, you're treated as making a contribution to the IRA. If you've already contributed the maximum amount, the added amount from paying brokerage commissions on behalf of your IRA will be an excess contribution that will result in penalties unless corrected.

Wrap fees. People with large IRAs sometimes invest them in programs that charge an overall fee, called a wrap fee, that covers investment advisory services, trading costs and other services provided in managing the account. The IRS issued a private letter ruling in February 2005 saying these fees could be treated like trustee fees; in other words, you can use money from outside your IRA to pay these amounts without being treated as making a contribution. Although this was a private ruling issued to an individual taxpayer, it seems likely that the IRS will apply the same reasoning to other taxpayers.

Prohibited investments

The tax law says certain investments aren't permitted in an IRA. For the most part these prohibitions are designed to make sure these retirement accounts are invested in productive assets like stocks and bonds. The following investments are prohibited:

- Artworks, rugs, antiques
- Gems, stamps, coins
- Alcoholic beverages

In addition, investments in metals are prohibited with certain exceptions, which the IRS describes as follows:

> Your IRA can invest in one, one-half, one-quarter, or one-tenth ounce U.S. gold coins, or one-ounce silver coins minted by the Treasury Department. It can also invest in certain platinum coins and certain gold, silver, palladium and platinum bullion.

Be sure to get an opinion from someone with knowledge of these rules before making investments that may fall into any of these categories.

Consequences of a prohibited investment. If you make a prohibited investment, the amount invested is treated as a distribution from the IRA, even while the assets remain inside the IRA. To the extent a distribution of cash in the same amount would produce taxable income or an early distribution penalty, the same will apply to this deemed distribution.

Other prohibited transactions

Certain other things you might do with an IRA are specifically designated as *prohibited transactions.* The consequences are severe. With an exception noted below (*IRA used as security*), any of these transactions will nuke your entire IRA, even if the transaction involves just a portion of the IRA. You're treated as if the entire balance of the IRA was distributed to you on the first day of the year in which the transaction occurred. If a distribution of the IRA on that day would produce taxable income, you have to report that income. If it would result in a 10% early distribution penalty, you're stuck with that as well. In fact, the IRS says (in Publication 590-A) that the account "stops being an IRA," which presumably means any subsequent income or gains in the account will be taxable, as if it were a regular investment account. These rules are designed to make you want to steer clear of anything that even vaguely resembles a prohibited transaction.

Related persons. Prohibited transaction rules generally apply not just to the owner of the IRA but also to related persons, including family members and also related entities such as partnerships, corporations and trusts. When we say, for example, that you aren't allowed to borrow money from your IRA, you can't avoid that rule by having your spouse or a company you own borrow from the IRA.

Borrowing from your IRA. Subject to certain restrictions, employers can allow participants to borrow from their 401k or 403b accounts, and many plans (though not all) include this feature. Borrowing from your own IRA is strictly prohibited, however. You can't do this even if the IRA was funded from a 401k or 403b rollover.

Some people are tempted to use the rollover rules to use money from an IRA for a short period of time. Those rules allow you to complete a rollover up to 60 days after you took the money out. There is no tracing rule, so you can spend the money immediately after a withdrawal and complete the rollover with funds from some other source. It's almost like getting a short-term loan from your IRA.

This is a dangerous strategy. The IRS is aware that people sometimes use the rollover rules as a way to borrow from an IRA, and they don't like the idea. Where the facts make it appear that this is the underlying reality, they've looked for ways to penalize the taxpayer, without necessarily invoking the prohibited transaction rules. For example, the IRS sometimes grants relief from the 60-day time limit for rollovers, but not if it appears that the taxpayer was using the rollover rules to borrow money from the IRA.

> Your IRA could lose protection from claims of creditors in bankruptcy if you use this technique. More than one IRA owner has lost his retirement savings when the court declared that the account no longer qualified as an IRA, and therefore no longer qualified for protection in bankruptcy, because the owner used the rollover rules to obtain the equivalent of a loan from his IRA.

Using the IRA as security. The rules also say you can't use the IRA as security for a loan you obtain elsewhere. In this case, if you use only a portion of the IRA as security for the loan, then the part of the IRA that's treated as a distribution is only that portion.

Buying from, or selling to, your IRA. You aren't allowed to buy anything from your IRA or sell anything to it. For example, if you own shares of stock in your regular brokerage account and decide it would be better for the IRA to own those shares, selling them to the IRA would be a prohibited transaction.

You also can't contribute the shares to your IRA, because all contributions except as part of a rollover or conversion have to be in cash.

Personal use property. You need a place to live and you have money in your IRA. Why not have the IRA buy a home where you can live? Because it's a prohibited transaction, that's why. Ditto if you're thinking the IRA could buy a home where relatives could live. Or a vacation home you'll use. These items may be legitimate investments, but personal use means they're prohibited for your IRA.

Providing services. Although the IRS doesn't mention this rule in its publication on IRAs, the tax law contains a prohibition against "furnishing goods, services or facilities" between an IRA and its owner. What catches my eye here is the word *services.* You're certainly allowed to do some things for your IRA—you can set it up, select investments, and monitor those investments, changing them from time to time. When you go beyond those actions, you risk having a prohibited transaction.

> **Example:** You buy real estate as an investment in your IRA. The property needs repairs, and you decide to perform those repairs yourself.

It seems to me that in this situation you're furnishing services to your IRA. Regardless of whether you charge your IRA for those services, the IRS may contend that you've engaged in a prohibited transaction, effectively terminating your IRA.

Wash sales

The *wash sale rule* is designed to prevent people from claiming a loss on a sale of stock if they buy replacement shares of the same stock at about the same time. The basic rule says you can't take the deduction if you buy the same stock within 30 days before or after the date of the sale. You don't have to worry about this rule when you're buying and selling stock within an IRA because there's no way to claim losses for those sales in any event. The reason we have an issue here is that some people get the bright idea that they can avoid the wash sale rule for sales in a regular investment account if they buy replacement shares in their IRA.

> **Example:** You have a stock investment that lost $5,000 of value and you would like to deduct that loss on your tax return. You can claim the loss if you sell the stock and avoid buying replacement shares for at least 31 days—but you think there's a good chance the stock will surge upward during that time frame. In an attempt to avoid the wash sale rule, you sell the stock in your regular investment account and use money in your IRA to buy replacement shares.

In 2008 the IRS issued guidance (Rev. Rul. 2008-5) confirming that a loss is not allowed in this situation. The ruling went on to say that you don't obtain basis in your IRA when the loss is disallowed. That means you can't claim the loss on the original sale, and you also can't use the loss to reduce the amount of income you report in connection with your IRA withdrawals. This is a harsh result, completely eliminating any tax benefit from the loss you suffered on your investment, so you should take care not to buy replacement shares in an IRA shortly before or after selling shares at a loss in a regular investment account.

Other transactions

Here are a couple of other ideas the IRS doesn't like:

Annuity valuation. The amount of income you report when you convert from a traditional to a Roth IRA depends on the value of the account at the time of the conversion. Some people apparently thought they could reduce the cost of a conversion by having the traditional account purchase an annuity, and then claiming the value of the annuity was limited to its cash surrender value at the time of the conversion, a number that does not reflect the full value of the annuity. The IRS responded by issuing regulations that set forth rules for determining the value of an annuity held in a traditional account at the time of a conversion. The value determined under these rules will typically be higher than the cash surrender value of the annuity.

Shifting value or income to a Roth. Taxpayers who find ways to shift income or value to a Roth IRA may eliminate tax they would otherwise pay on gains or income. The IRS identified one type of transaction being used by some taxpayers, where the Roth IRA would own a corporation, and the IRA owner, or a related person (or related business), would enter into a transaction that was favorable to that corporation, such as a sale of business receivables at an unreasonably low price. Transactions of this type carry the potential for treatment as prohibited transactions, resulting in termination of the IRA as described earlier. In addition, the IRS has placed them in a special category called *listed transactions*, a term that implies the potential for harsh penalties on anyone involved, including people who promote the strategy.

27

Investing Your Retirement Account

Here's a sound approach to long-term investing.

MANY PEOPLE FACE THE DAUNTING TASK of choosing their investments without the benefit of professional advice. Even if you seek help from a professional, it may be difficult to know you're receiving sound, unbiased advice. Everyone who has a retirement account should take the time to learn the fundamentals of investing.

My book on investing, *That Thing Rich People Do*, provides a short, painless explanation of the key principles. This chapter summarizes the essentials.

Types of investments

Let's begin by making sure we're familiar with the types of investments that make sense for retirement investing. Here's a brief description of the main categories.

Stocks. Stocks give you an opportunity to become a part owner of the company issuing the shares. Dividends paid on those shares can make your money grow, but usually the more important factor is growth in the value of the shares themselves. You can buy stocks directly but it usually makes sense to buy them through *mutual funds*, which are described later, under *Diversification*. Over short periods of time stocks can lose value, but over long periods of time they have outperformed other types of investments by a wide margin.

Bonds. Bonds are issued by companies or governments (including the U.S. government) as a way to borrow money. When you buy a bond you place yourself in the position of being a lender, receiving interest on the money loaned to the issuer. Over the long haul, money invested in bonds can be expected to grow more slowly than money invested in stocks, but with less fluctuation. Here again you can invest directly or through mutual funds.

Certificates of deposit. These are similar to bonds. You're lending money to a bank or other financial institution in return for interest payments.

Money markets. Money market funds (or money market *accounts*) are similar to bond investments, earning interest on money loaned to companies or governments, but the loans are for such short periods of time that they involve almost no risk of losing value. Unfortunately, they also provide no chance to earn good returns.

Stable value funds. These are available in many 401k plans. They strive to offer the higher returns of bonds with the lower risks of money market funds. It's too soon to know how these relatively new funds will perform over the long term, but it seems reasonable to expect both risk and return to fall somewhere between the levels for money market funds and bond funds.

> Some descriptions of stable value funds create the misleading impression that they involve no investment risk at all. Zero risk simply isn't possible, and certain types of events may cause these funds to perform worse than money market funds.

Real estate. A direct purchase of real estate in a retirement account rarely makes sense, but you may wish to put some of your money in a *real estate investment trust* (*REIT*), which is like a mutual fund except that it invests in real property or mortgages.

Other. There are other choices of course, but generally they are not suitable for retirement investing. People invest in all kinds of things from soybean futures to fine art, but if you're interested in a financially secure retirement you'll want to focus on items like those on the list above.

Four principles

Although investing is a huge subject matter, you can secure good long-term performance with a focus on just four principles. They don't require a great deal of learning, but they do require discipline. Obey these principles and you'll avoid major disasters. What's more, if you stick with them over a long period of time you'll be assured of doing far better than the average investor. Here they are:

- *Saving.* A regular, disciplined program of saving is the starting point for building retirement wealth.

- *Asset allocation.* You need to put your money in the right kinds of investments, such as stocks and bonds.
- *Diversification.* Your investments—especially your stock investments—need to be well diversified.
- *Expenses.* Your investment expenses must be as low as possible.

People that fail in any one of these areas can end up with a poor investment outcome. Sticking with all four will eliminate the major sources of disaster. We'll look at each of these principles, and then consider how various investment alternatives can serve your needs.

Saving

You can't begin the process of investing if you don't have money to invest, and for most of us that means we have to be saving on a regular basis. There are countless books offering tips on how to cut down on your spending, often with a pep talk to help with the motivation. My personal favorite in this category is a perennial best-seller from Andrew Tobias called *The Only Investment Guide You'll Ever Need.* As the title indicates, the book also covers other aspects of investing. Start with that one and then poke around your local library, bookstore or Internet if you need more help.

Saving money is as much a matter of personal attitude as it is a matter of technique. It's hard to say how effective any single book can be in changing lifelong habits of thought, but many people find *The Richest Man in Babylon* by George S. Clason to be a real eye-opener. It's also a quick, easy, fun book to read. Another book that offers a good healthy whack on the side of the head is *The Millionaire Next Door* by Stanley and Danko.

My only piece of advice in this area is one you'll see just about everywhere: set up a system of automatic payments into your retirement account. The normal way to fund a 401k or 403b account is through payroll deductions, so that's easy. It takes only a little more effort do the same thing with an IRA. At many companies the payroll department will send a portion of your paycheck directly to an account you designate. Otherwise you can tell the IRA provider to take an automatic withdrawal from your checking account each month.

These automatic payments take a lot of the pain out of saving and, more importantly, take a lot of the "forget" out of saving as well. What's more, many IRA providers offer a smaller minimum amount to start an account if you set up automatic payments. You just have to remember to boost the amount you're saving every year or two as your income grows.

Regular saving produces another benefit when the money goes into investments that can fluctuate in value, such as stocks. There's no way to predict the short-term ups and downs, but you can use them to your advantage when you add the same dollar amount to your savings on a regular basis. When prices dip lower, the shares don't cost as much so your fixed dollar amount buys more shares. A higher price means your fixed amount will buy fewer shares. The purchase price of the shares you bought ends up being better than average because you bought more shares at the low prices than at the high prices. This phenomenon, called *dollar cost averaging*, improves your investment performance without requiring any brainpower other than setting up periodic additions to your savings.

Asset allocation

It rarely makes sense to put all your retirement savings in any one category of investments. A key step in the thought process is to decide what percentage of the total will go into each type of investment. This is called *asset allocation*. Failure to establish and maintain a good asset allocation is one of the places many investors make costly mistakes.

Stocks. Begin with stocks. How much of your account will be invested in the stock market, either directly or through mutual funds? For some people the answer is zero. They understand that stock prices move up and down, and can't stomach the possibility of losing some of the hard-earned money they poured into their retirement accounts.

Yet over long periods of time stocks have outperformed other types of investments by a wide margin. They've done better than bonds. Better than real estate. *Way* better than money markets or precious metals. Investing without stocks is like driving in first gear. You may be moving forward but most of the world is passing you by.

> For details on the extent to which stocks have overpowered other investments read Jeremy Siegel's best-selling book, *Stocks for the Long Run.*

In the end you have to be comfortable with the investments you make. It won't help for you to put money into stocks if you'll chicken out and sell the investments the first time the stock market takes one of its customary dips. What's more, an investment that puts you in a panic isn't good for your quality of life. But try to understand that you aren't eliminating risk when you stay out of the stock market. You're exchanging one risk for another: the risk that your "safe" investments will grow too slowly to provide financial security in your retirement.

Apart from your risk tolerance, the percentage you allocate to stocks should depend in part on your age. If the past is any guide (admittedly, a big if), you can be comfortable in expecting a good stock investment to perform well over very long periods of time. Over shorter periods, even a well-managed stock portfolio can lose value, taking years to recover. The standard advice is to invest more heavily in stocks when you're young, dialing back as you move toward retirement. In your twenties and thirties, and even into your forties, it can be reasonable to put 80% or more of your retirement savings into stocks if you're comfortable with that much risk. (You don't have to go that high if you don't want. You can put 60% in stocks and still play a winning game.) A smaller percentage makes sense for most people in their fifties and sixties. Because of increased life expectancies, though, many advisors recommend keeping a substantial part of a retirement fund in stocks even after age 65.

Other investments. Include other investments in your retirement account with the goal of reducing the risk you experience from your stock investments without reducing performance too much. Over the long haul, bonds don't perform as well as stocks, but they can offer reasonable returns while taming the wild swings you would experience if you put all your money in stocks. You can get a lot of risk reduction bang for your buck when you include at least a small percentage of bonds in your account because bonds sometimes do quite well at precisely the same time stocks are taking a dive. The same is true of real estate investment trusts (REITs). It would make sense to put most of the non-stock part of your account into bonds, and perhaps a smaller chunk into a REIT (or fund of REITs) if that's available.

A money market fund or account is a great place to stuff a pile of cash you're planning to use in the near future. You don't want the money you'll need for next April's tax bill, or next September's tuition bill, exposed to the stock market's swings. Money market funds allow you to pick up some interest on that money without having to worry about whether it will still be there when you need it. Certificates of deposit can serve the same function.

Within a retirement plan, the main function of these low-return investments is to push risk to a lower level than you can achieve when moving part of your account from stocks into bonds. Depending on your age and risk tolerance, that's fine up to a point. But these funds produce earnings so paltry that during some periods they don't even keep pace with inflation. That's worse than driving in first gear. You're locked in neutral and sliding backwards. Stable value funds may be a little better because of their higher returns, but you may need to rethink your strategy if you're putting most or all your retirement savings into these low-yielding investments.

Diversification

To be well diversified, your stock holdings must be divided among many different stocks. More than that, they must be divided among many different *kinds* of stocks. You've probably heard this before. Are you a believer?

Many people have a hard time accepting the need for diversification. Common sense tells them there's less risk in holding a single good stock about which they have plenty of information (such as stock in the company where they work) than holding a lot of different stocks about which they know little. Well, common sense also tells us the earth is flat and stands still while the sun passes overhead. Diversification is one of the most important principles in investing. Let's see why.

Where risk comes from. Stock prices are determined by the buying and selling activity that goes on in the stock market, where billions of shares change hands every day. Everyone involved is trying to maximize profits.

Imagine what would happen if we had an objective, reliable way to determine stock performance. No one would be willing to buy a stock that's set to fall unless sellers lowered the price to a level that reflects that decline. No one would be willing to sell a stock that's set to rise unless buyers raised the price to a level that compensates for the increase.

This is precisely what happens in the stock market every day. Buyers and sellers constantly adjust prices to reflect everything that is known, and everything that can be predicted. Good news won't make the stock go up unless it truly is *news.* An increase in profits or the announcement of a wonderful new product won't change the price if investors were able to predict the development, because the "news" is already built into the price of the stock.

> Stock prices gravitate toward a level at which objective, reliable predictions are not possible, and as a result, price movements are largely random.

It may seem logical that you can moderate this risk by keeping a close eye on the stock. That doesn't work. You have no way of knowing whether a small drop in the stock price is a temporary dip along the way to a new high or the start of a devastating decline. By the time a bad situation becomes clear you're likely to think the stock has reached a bargain price from which recovery seems certain, so you hold on while it falls further. Enron shareholders didn't lose money because they failed to keep an eye on the stock. They watched it and watched it and watched it until there was nothing left to watch.

How diversification reduces risk. If each individual stock is affected by significant randomness, we can see that there is quite a bit of risk when you invest in any single stock. An interesting thing happens when you divide your money between two different stocks, though. There will be days when they both go up, and days when they both go down, but there will also be days when one goes up and the other goes down. Even when they both go down, one will lose ground less than the other, reducing the sharpness of the decline. Random fluctuations partly cancel each other out. You get more and more cancellation when you invest in more and more stocks, especially if they represent companies in diverse segments of the economy.

You can't eliminate all the risk, of course, because there are some random fluctuations that affect the overall stock market. A common measure of fluctuation called *volatility* is usually measured around 18% for the overall stock market. For an individual stock, it can easily be two or three times as high—or more. A single stock isn't just a little bit riskier than a diversified portfolio. It's completely off the charts.

Here's the real bonus in diversification: it reduces risk without reducing your returns. If you take two different stocks that should produce an average return of 10% and put them in the same account, you get a portfolio that should produce an average return of 10%. You didn't give up anything in the way of performance, but you're exposed to less risk than if you held either stock by itself, because of the cancelling effect described earlier. Put in a bunch more 10% stocks and you reduce the risk even more, but you still get 10% average performance from the portfolio.

This means the added risk from failing to diversify is an especially ugly kind of risk. Normally, if you're willing to take more risk, you're rewarded with a higher average return. That's what happens when you move from a money market fund to bonds, or when you move from bonds to stocks. Failure to diversify increases your level of risk without doing anything to increase your returns. In the language of the finance professors, it exposes you to *uncompensated risk*. It's also unnecessary risk, unwise risk.

Have you ever heard someone moan about a major disaster in investing? *My 401k turned into a 201k*. Failure to diversify is nearly always at the heart of the problem. You can suffer losses in a well-diversified account, but you're a lot less likely to experience the kind of debacle that alters your standard of living in a meaningful way. So please, make sure your investments are diversified.

> Diversifying is like wearing a seatbelt: it provides added safety without slowing you down. It won't keep you out of an accident (or investment losses) but you're a lot more likely to survive.

Good diversification. Good diversification isn't simply a matter of dividing your investments among a large number of stocks. You need to hold different *kinds* of stocks. Most importantly, you need to hold stocks in different segments of the economy, even if you're mainly interested in one particular segment, such as the one where you work. Sorry if this means some of your stock holdings will seem to be boring. When it comes to avoiding investment losses, boring is good.

Here's a vivid example of the difference between good and bad diversification. During a particularly ugly 2½-year period beginning in March 2000, the Dow Jones Industrial Average, consisting of 30 stocks, fell more than 30%. During the same period, the Nasdaq index, consisting of a much larger number of stocks, fell more than *80%*. This huge disparity occurred because the Nasdaq is heavily loaded with technology stocks, the ones that were hit worst in the bear market. The Dow includes technology stocks, too, but also includes McDonald's and American Express and Disney and Wal-Mart, stocks that held up a lot better while stocks like Intel were getting hammered. The Dow has fewer stocks, but it's better diversified than the Nasdaq.

Individual stocks. If you hold your retirement savings in a brokerage account you can build a well-diversified portfolio out of individual stocks. This approach requires considerable skill, however. What's more, because of the costs involved, it's unlikely to be the best approach unless you have a great deal more wealth than the average person saving for retirement.

Mutual funds. Fortunately, there's an easy, inexpensive way to accomplish good stock diversification. *Mutual funds* sell shares to investors and use the money to invest in a portfolio. People holding shares in the mutual fund get an investment result based on the performance of that portfolio. You make just one purchase—the mutual fund shares—and you end up indirectly owning stock in a large number of companies.

You don't necessarily get *good* diversification when you buy mutual fund shares, however. Some of these funds specialize in a particular kind of stocks. For example, there are mutual funds that invest only in the stocks of the Nasdaq index, providing a heavy dose of technology stocks and not enough in other sectors to ease the pain when the market for high tech stocks turns sour. Many others focus on particular segments of the economy or particular types of stocks. No matter how hot or exciting those funds sound, they should not be more than a very small portion of your retirement account. Your core holdings should be well balanced.

That doesn't mean you have to own a large number of mutual funds. You can get good diversification within a single mutual fund if it's the kind that invests in all parts of the economy. If your 401k or 403b plan offers many different stock funds you may feel you should spread your money around among them, but that isn't always the best choice.

The goal is to own some things that will perform well when other parts of your portfolio are going south. That's part of the attraction of owning bonds or REITs. You don't buy them because they'll be the best performers in your account, but rather because they can move in the opposite direction of your stocks, the real engine of growth.

Investment expenses

The last of the four key principles of investing is to minimize your investment expenses. Over the long haul, seemingly small differences in the expense levels can make a huge difference in your wealth.

> **Example:** An investor started with $20,000 in a retirement account and after 36 years of investing produced an average return of 9.5% per year, before taking into account expenses of 2.5% per year. The result was 7% annual growth and an ending value of $228,000.
>
> Another investor managed the same growth rate over the same period of time but shaved expenses to 1.5% per year. The result was 8% annual growth and an ending value of nearly $320,000.
>
> A third investor also produced 9.5% growth while being relentless in minimizing investment expenses, keeping them to 0.5% per year. The result was 9% annual growth and an ending value of $445,000.

The expense levels in this example are well within the range experienced by different investors. Many are unaware of the high expense levels they're experiencing, or mistakenly believe their high-expense approach will lead to higher returns. The results in the example above speak for themselves.

You can't completely eliminate investment expenses, but you can avoid many situations that can make them higher than necessary. Here are some of the most important culprits:

- Frequent trading in a portfolio of stocks greatly reduces the returns from the portfolio. This is true even if you use a discount broker with low commissions.

- There's a wide range of expense levels among mutual funds, and little evidence that the ones with higher expenses produce higher returns.
- Expenses associated with variable annuities are often extremely high.

You'll have a much greater chance of reaching your goals if you minimize your investment expenses.

> Now that we've covered the four key principles of investing we can look at types of investments that may or may not help you reach your goals.

Your company's stock

Many companies offer their own stock as one of the investments in a 401k plan. Special considerations, good and bad, apply to this investment.

On the good side, you aren't a purely passive investor. Instead of merely hoping your investments increase in value, you're doing something about it as you perform your daily duties. You aren't just an employee any more; you're a partner, someone who shares in the success of the business. Anyway, investing is more fun when you know something about the companies in which you invest. Owning shares of the company where you work can add to the satisfaction you get from your job and from your investments.

The big negative is risk. In a purely objective analysis, it's actually worse to own a lot of stock of the company where you work than any other company. A key principle of good risk management is to avoid situations where a single unfortunate event can have many bad consequences. If something really bad happens to the company where you work, it can affect your compensation or even your job security. If you've loaded up on the company's stock, your retirement account is getting hit at the same time. You may also be losing value in your home, either because you're forced to move or because the company's troubles are affecting the local economy. The events that could lead to this scenario may seem unlikely, but they happen more often than you might think, and they are never expected by the company's workers.

If you like the idea of owning company stock, I see nothing wrong with devoting a small portion of your account to this investment. The point would be to gain the advantages mentioned above while keeping risk at an acceptable level. If company stock represents less than 10% of your retirement savings, a disastrous loss of value in that stock will not be a life-changing event. Once you move above that level you expose yourself to the possibility that a single adverse development will produce losses from which you can't recover, forcing you to delay retirement or permanently reducing your standard of living.

Many people have a hard time accepting the notion that a large investment in their own company can be bad, especially if the company has been scoring strong successes and the stock price has gone up. Remember that the company and the stock are two different things. If investors become overly optimistic, the stock price can reach an unjustifiably high level, after which it may fall even while the company is performing well. And unexpected events, perhaps outside the control of anyone at the company, can unleash a whirlwind that wipes out an astonishing amount of value before people can react.

> Putting too much money in your company's stock means you aren't well diversified, violating one of the key principles of investing.

Index investing

Index investing is an idea that sounds strange at first—so strange that many people reject the idea before they have a chance to learn why it makes sense. It's perfectly reasonable for you to decide index investing isn't for you, but you should understand its advantages before you discard the notion. Index investing offers a way to do significantly better than most other investors. Here's a brief summary of the reasons.

How it works. Start with the idea of an index. It tells us the average performance of all investors holding shares of any or all companies in a particular list of stocks. Some investors will do better than the index and some do worse, but the index tells us the result you would get if you added them all together and treated them as one big megainvestor.

When someone says the market went up 100 points, they're usually referring to the Dow Jones Industrial Average, which actually measures the performance of just 30 stocks. The S&P 500 comes closer to measuring the overall performance of the market. As the name suggests, it covers 500 stocks. That's fewer than 10% of all U.S. stocks, but these are, roughly speaking, the 500 *largest* U.S. stocks, and they represent about 70% of the total value of the U.S. stock market. Another index, called the Dow Jones Wilshire 5000, covers all U.S. stocks with readily available prices (actually more than 5,000 stocks). There are many other indexes designed to measure stocks in various categories.

Mutual funds that invest in stocks can be divided into two categories. *Managed* funds have managers that try to select stocks that will perform better than others. *Index* funds don't even try to beat the index. They simply try to *match* the index. The basic approach is to hold all the stocks in the index, in the appropriate percentages so that the value of the mutual fund shares will rise or fall at the same rate as the index.

If you think that's a strange approach to investing, you're not alone. It seems obvious that any list of stocks will include some that are going to perform better than others. Even if we can't come up with entirely reliable predictions, it seems like we should be able to do better than average if we apply some intelligence to the selection of better stocks. Anyway, how can you possibly do better than average by *matching* the average?

Winners and losers. In the town of Lake Wobegon, according to Garrison Keillor, all the children are above average. In the stock market, that's a mathematical impossibility. Every dollar of above average performance by one person is matched by a dollar of below average performance by someone else. That's the whole idea behind creating an average in the first place, to show the midpoint in performance.

Those dollars of below average performance aren't going to come from index investors, because those folks are investing in a way that matches the relevant average almost exactly. The losers have to come from the same group that produced the winners: investors that are *not* investing in the index.

By and large, everyone that doesn't invest in the index is hoping to do better than the index. What's more, the bulk of the money invested in the market is managed by skilled professionals. There are of course millions of individual investors, some of whom buy and sell stocks without having the skill to do it well, but they represent a small fraction of the overall wealth invested in the market, and even in that group you'll find people who perform above average.

What this means is that a lot of the below-average performance—most of it, in fact—has to come from investments that are managed by skilled professionals, trying as hard as they can to do *better* than average. Thoughtful management of your investments does not assure above average performance. It can have just the opposite result.

On average, people who are trying to beat the market do no better than index investors, who *don't* try to beat the market.

The same logic that applies to stock picking applies to the task of picking a winning mutual fund or other investment manager. Common sense tells us that all investors seek to put money only in funds that will perform better than average. If we knew ahead of time which funds will outperform the others, all our money would go into those funds. But then the losing funds wouldn't exist and we'd be left with a situation where all the funds are above average, like the children of Lake Wobegon.

How indexing wins. At this point we have a picture of how index investors can do just as well as other investors. How can they do better? Two words: lower expenses. Make it three: *much* lower expenses.

I won't take the space here to describe all these expenses, which include sales charges (or *loads*), management fees and trading costs among others. For present purposes it is enough to know that when you add them all up, they can take a painfully large slice out of the performance of managed investments. Index funds incur expenses too, but at much lower levels.

To do better than an index fund, it isn't enough for a managed fund to pick stocks that perform better than average. It has to outperform the market by a wide enough margin to cover all the added expenses of this kind of investing. That's a tough task, considering that as a practical matter, a manager's above average performance has to come as the result of underperformance by another highly skilled investment professional.

Bottom line. The world of managed investing consists largely of smart people being paid a lot of money to outsmart one another. Some people come out ahead but a majority do not. Index investors observe the battle quietly from the sidelines and, on average, grow their money much faster than investors who try to beat the market. Index investing isn't for everyone, but it's a sensible approach and, in the final analysis, one that's hard to beat.

Managed mutual funds

If you decide against index investing, you'll want to choose one or more managed funds that provide good diversification while offering a reasonable chance to outperform a comparable index fund. Bear in mind that *everyone* tries to select the funds that will perform best. Here are some thoughts on selecting a mutual fund.

"Past performance is no guarantee . . ." Many people choose mutual funds the way they would choose players for a fantasy baseball team: pick the ones that had the best batting average or ERA last year, hoping they'll repeat that performance. It seems logical to suppose that last year's investment stars will hit it out of the park again this year. Things don't work that way in the stock market, though. In fact, odd as it may sound, you should be especially cautious about investing with a mutual fund that recently produced astoundingly good results.

One problem is that it's extremely difficult to tell how much of an investment manager's success is attributable to skill as opposed to style. During a period when growth stocks are performing well, a manager whose style favors these stocks can produce a good record even without unusually strong stock picking skills. Next year may not be such a great year for growth stocks—you can never tell in advance—and the same manager may falter, like a good fastball hitter suddenly facing a lot of knuckleballs.

Once in a while a mutual fund manager appears to be a genuine stock market genius. Then another issue crops up. Investors flood that mutual fund with money, creating a strange problem: too much money to invest. It's always possible to invest more money, of course, but when you're dealing with huge sums it becomes harder to invest profitably. Your uncanny ability to spot a little gem of a company that's likely to double in value doesn't help much if the company is so small it will account for a miniscule percentage of your portfolio. Even when you invest in larger companies, your purchases are so huge that they can cause a temporary bump in the stock price, forcing you to pay a premium to establish your position in that stock. In this business, success sows the seeds of future futility.

Extreme success in a mutual fund over a short period of time is a warning that the mutual fund may be using a high-risk investment approach. Time and again, mutual funds that performed at the very top of their category in one year become among the worst performers a year or two later. Think twice before committing a large portion of your retirement account to a fund that crushed its competitors by a wide margin.

What to look for. You shouldn't completely ignore past performance, of course. Look for funds that have done reasonably well over a number of years. Remember to evaluate that performance relative to how the overall stock market is doing. In a typical year you should be happy with 10% growth, but that would be a poor result in a year the market went up 15%. Likewise, a modest loss can be an excellent result in a year the stock market falls sharply. Don't expect to find a fund that beats the market every year, but favor the ones that avoid wild swings relative to the performance of the market. Stability in the management of the fund is important, too. A fund may have trouble continuing a stellar record after losing the manager that produced that record.

If there's a single factor tends to sort out the good funds from the rest, it is expenses. Funds that have high expense ratios and rapid turnover of their investments are rarely able to sustain the superior performance required to justify those costs. You greatly improve your chances of success if you choose mutual funds where the expenses are lower than average.

Annuities

Annuities are contracts with insurance companies that promise to make a stream of payments, usually for the lifetime of the owner of the policy, or the joint lives of that person and his or her spouse. Their main purpose is the opposite of life insurance. Instead of providing money to replace lost income if you die earlier than expected, an annuity prevents you from running out of money if you live longer than expected.

The simplest form of annuity is called an *immediate fixed annuity*. The amount of the monthly payout is determined at the time you buy the annuity (which is why it's *fixed*), and payments begin right after you buy it (which is why it's *immediate*). People often buy this type of annuity around the time they retire, using a portion of their retirement savings. There's no need to buy ahead of time: unlike life insurance, an annuity won't become less affordable (or less available) as you grow older.

Most experts agree that an immediate fixed annuity can make sense for many people. Another type, called a *variable annuity*, is more controversial. These may be purchased years before the stream of payments will be needed, with part of the purchase price invested in *subaccounts* that function like mutual funds. The size of the payment stream will depend on the performance of these subaccounts. Many offerings have features designed to make them seem more attractive, such as protection against certain losses.

The main problem is that many variable annuities are laden with expenses so high as to virtually guarantee inferior investment performance. What's more, they often require buyers to pay costly surrender charges if they want to move their money to a different investment.

Variable annuities are not universally bad. The low-cost ones that are likely to perform best are not the ones that are most heavily promoted, however. Take your time when considering a purchase, and if possible, obtain an independent opinion. The opportunity to buy won't disappear.

Bad investment ideas

It would be impossible to create a catalog of all the bad investment ideas that are floating around. Here are just a few that have been promoted for retirement accounts.

Day trading. Through the Fairmark.com web site I've come into contact with many people who tried to make money rapidly buying and selling stocks. Almost all of them lost large sums, from tens of thousands of dollars up into the millions. The only sense in which this is better than flushing money down the toilet is you don't have to worry about clogged pipes.

Derivatives. Stock options, commodity futures, currency futures and similar items are collectively known as *derivatives* because their value is derived from the value of some other asset. They have two things in common:

- They generate handsome fees for the people who sell them.
- They often produce stunning losses for amateur speculators looking for quick profits.

Some people make money on these investments, at least for a while, just as some people leave a casino richer than they went in. As in a casino, losses are all but inevitable if you play the game more than a short period of time.

Penny stocks. Companies that don't qualify for trading on the major stock exchanges can still offer shares to the public. These shares often trade for less than $1.00, so they're called *penny stocks*. It's hard to get reliable information on these stocks, and they're frequent targets of abusive schemes. Spreads and other costs of investing tend to be much higher than for regular stocks. In short, this is a lousy way to invest. Remember the old saying: penny stock, pound foolish.

Real estate. The direct purchase of real estate in an IRA isn't illegal and it isn't a scam, but it's almost always a bad idea. People pitching this idea usually have something to sell, such as pricy seminars where they teach you the ropes or services connected with maintaining an IRA that holds real estate. They often skimp on warnings about potential problems, instead protecting themselves with a notice telling you to consult with your own advisor, knowing full well that few of their potential customers will take this action. Here are some of the key things you won't learn from the promoters.

To begin with, if you're a homeowner you already have a large investment in real estate. One of the most important principles of investing is to avoid overexposure to a single class of assets. You're almost surely violating that principle if you buy real estate in a retirement account. A cycle of bad performance in the real estate market would cause your retirement account to lose value at the same time your home is faring poorly.

An equally important principle is to be diversified within each asset class. Few people have enough wealth to maintain their own diversified portfolio of real estate investments. If your money is tied up in a few properties, a single event could result in a loss that will alter your standard of living.

In any case, a retirement account simply isn't a good vehicle for real estate investing:

- Outside an IRA you can obtain various tax benefits for holding real estate. Those benefits are unavailable for real estate held in an IRA.
- Outside an IRA you can hold real estate for years without ever having to get it appraised. You may be forced to determine the value of real estate held in an IRA to comply with the tax rules.
- Outside an IRA you have complete freedom to add more money to an existing real estate investment. You can't simply add money to an IRA if one of its properties needs a new roof.
- Outside an IRA you can perform work on your own property, use it for personal purposes, or make it available for the use of family members or a business you own. These actions can result in prohibited transactions for property held in an IRA.

Direct ownership of real estate in an IRA is awkward and expensive. If you feel that real property is the best way to invest your retirement money, buy shares of REITs, or a mutual fund that holds REIT shares. These real estate investments provide diversification and professional management. They're the only sensible way to own real estate in a retirement account.

A simple approach

If you're a little confused after reading this much, here's a simple way to approach the problem of investing your retirement account.

First, you'll want to focus on mutual funds. In a 401k or 403b account these are likely to be the main offerings, if not the only ones. You have more choice for an IRA, including the opportunity to make your own selections of individual stocks. Unless you've developed professional-level investment expertise, though, you're better off sticking with mutual funds, at least for the core investments that make up most of your savings.

Before you select particular mutual funds, determine what portion should go into each type of investment, beginning with stocks. As discussed earlier, stocks can lose money in the short run, but have outperformed other kinds of investments when we look at long periods of time. Assuming your retirement fund is a long-term investment, it makes sense to put a substantial part of it in stocks. If you're under 50 years of age, you can reasonably put 80% or more into a diversified stock investment if the risk won't make you lose sleep. You'll want to dial back the stock investment at an older age, but bear in mind that even at age 60 a normal life expectancy is long enough so that a substantial investment in stocks continues to make sense. Your primary investment for the non-stock portion of the fund, and perhaps the only one you need, would be bonds, because they dampen the risk of holding stocks without lowering your returns as much as an ultra-safe investment like a money market fund.

Once you've decided on your percentages for stocks and bonds, look for mutual fund investments that produce that result. One way is to look for a single mutual fund that has the right mix, providing a good investment while keeping your life as simple as possible. There are two types of funds that let you do this.

- *Balanced funds* invest part of their money in stocks and part in bonds. The balance isn't necessarily 50-50, though. Many invest about 60% in stocks, and others use different ratios. Read the fund's prospectus to see if its ratio matches your preference.

- *Target retirement funds* are similar to balanced funds, but are designed to automatically cut back on stocks as their investors move closer to retirement. You choose a fund that's appropriate for your age or projected retirement date, and then forget about it. The fund will adjust the percentages gradually over a period of time in a way that makes sense for people your age.

You can also create the desired percentage of stocks and bonds by dividing your money between stock mutual funds and bond mutual funds. In this case you'll have to adjust the investments from time to time to keep the percentages appropriate. Stocks tend to move in spurts, racing ahead during some periods and falling back during others. If your money is in a balanced fund or a life cycle fund, the manager will make appropriate adjustments to maintain the proper ratios. If you created your own mix from different types of funds, you'll have to do this *rebalancing* yourself.

Rebalancing to a consistent ratio provides an added benefit. Besides maintaining proper ratios, it forces you to buy stocks after they've gone down and sell them after they've gone up—in other words, buy low and sell high, the classic formula for stock market success.

It's largely a matter of taste whether you go with index funds or managed funds. As discussed earlier, you're likely to do better with index funds, but many people can't let go of the idea they should be striving to outperform the market. When it comes to selecting particular funds, the most important principles are good diversification and low expenses. Stick with these and you're likely to do much better than people who chase after funds that recently produced spectacular performance.

Allocation among accounts

If you have a regular investment account in addition to your IRA or 401k account, you don't necessarily have to keep a good balance between stocks, bonds and other investments in each account. For example, if you have two accounts that are of equal size and you've decided to keep 70% of your money invested in the stock market, you can accomplish that goal by investing each account 70% in stocks, but you could also invest all of one account in stocks and add just enough stock investments in the other account to bring the total up to 70%.

That raises an interesting question: which type of account is best for which type of investment? The answer isn't entirely clear.

One approach is to look at the ongoing tax cost of holding an asset in a taxable account. Bonds produce interest income, which is taxed at ordinary tax rates. The same is true for much of the dividend income produced by REITs. On the other hand, stocks produce capital gains and qualifying dividends, both of which are taxed at favorable rates. The tax cost of holding stock in a taxable account is smaller than the tax cost of holding bonds there, so the strategy of holding stocks in the taxable account seems to make sense. You would keep bonds, REITs, and any other assets that throw off ordinary income in the retirement account.

Over the long haul, though, stock investments grow faster than bonds or other investments. If you keep stocks in your taxable account, chances are this account will grow faster than the retirement account. Studies published some years ago suggest that the long-term benefit of having greater growth in a retirement account can outstrip the short-term detriment of paying a higher rate of tax on investment income. Based on this theory, it might be better to keep stocks in the retirement account.

Many of these studies were published before the recent reductions in tax rates for long-term capital gains and qualifying dividends, however. At least one recent study finds that under current law you'll come out better if you keep stocks in your taxable account. In other words, we're back to the first thought, minimizing the ongoing tax cost of your investments.

Ultimately, any such study has to rely on educated guesses about future growth rates of different classes of investments, possible changes in the tax law, and how long the accounts will exist. Your personal style of investing will affect the result, and so will luck. I'm inclined to believe you shouldn't worry too much about this issue, but if you have a convenient opportunity to allocate stock investments to one type of account, I would choose the taxable account, and keep investments that produce ordinary income (such as bonds) in the retirement account.

If you're doing such an allocation, you should determine how much of each asset class (stocks, bonds, other) you're going to hold overall, and then determine where you're going to hold these investments. Don't let the size of your retirement account or the size of your taxable account determine the mix of investments.

> **Example:** The total amount in your investment accounts is $100,000. Of that amount, $25,000 is in a taxable account and $75,000 is in a Roth IRA. You've determined that you want 60% of your money invested in stocks and 40% in bonds.

It may make sense to invest the entire taxable account in stocks, and also invest $35,000 of the IRA in stocks so that the total stock investment matches your desired proportion. This approach is likely to reduce the amount of tax you pay on investment earnings of your taxable account. It would be a mistake, though, to invest the entire IRA in bonds simply because you won't pay tax on the IRA's investment earnings. You wouldn't have the correct overall ratio of stocks and bonds. Maintaining that ratio is more important than keeping a particular type of asset in one type of account.

28

Rollovers and Direct Transfers

Here's guidance on moving money from one retirement account to another.

IN PART IV WE SAW THAT YOU CAN MOVE MONEY or other assets from a traditional account to a Roth IRA in a conversion. This chapter deals with other kinds of transfers of money or assets from one retirement account to another:

- From one IRA to another, or from an IRA to an employer plan.
- From an employer plan to an IRA, or to an account in your new employer's plan.

Importance of these rules

The rules discussed in this chapter make it possible to move an account from one place to another. Often the goal is to gain access to better investments, lower fees or better service. More important is the opportunity to preserve tax benefits, especially when leaving a job where you've built up a retirement account.

All too often though, people fail to take advantage of this opportunity. Every year, countless participants in employer plans leave their jobs and take money from their accounts *without* rolling or transferring it to an IRA or to a new plan. It's understandable that this would happen, as many of these individuals receive the distributions at a time when they're incurring expenses associated with a change in employment, or perhaps dealing with a period of unemployment. Yet the opportunity cost is enormous. These funds represent money that can produce tax-deferred or tax-free earnings for decades to come. Failure to roll the money to an IRA or to a new employer account does away with that opportunity. Adding insult to injury, you may pay a 10% early distribution penalty on top of any regular income tax that applies to this distribution.

> Preserving your retirement account after a change in employment may be difficult, but it can be one of the most important financial moves you make.

Rollovers vs. direct transfers

When you move money from one retirement account to another, you often have a choice between two different methods. In a *rollover*, you receive a distribution of cash or other assets from the account and, within 60 days, deposit the money into a different retirement account. In a *direct transfer*, also called a *trustee-to-trustee transfer*, money or assets move directly from the trustee of the old retirement account to the trustee of the new one, untouched by human hands. This may seem like an unimportant distinction, but you should be aware of important differences in the two methods. Direct transfers are usually the preferred method:

- In a direct transfer, you don't have to worry about missing the 60-day deadline for completing a rollover.
- The rule requiring a one-year wait between rollovers doesn't apply to direct transfers.
- A direct transfer can eliminate the need for income tax withholding when the source of the rollover is a retirement plan maintained by an employer, rather than an IRA.
- When moving a Roth account from one employer plan to another, a direct transfer preserves the aging of the account, helping you satisfy the five-year requirement for qualified distributions. A rollover requires you to re-start the five-year clock.

You may find that you can avoid paying a fee to the trustee of your old IRA by doing a rollover instead of a trustee-to-trustee transfer. In that case a rollover may be the preferred method. More often, though, you're better off using a direct transfer.

When account moves are possible

The tax rules don't provide complete freedom to move money from one account to another whenever you want. You need to be in a position to take money from the old account, and the distribution has to be one you're allowed to roll to a new one.

IRA to IRA. You're always allowed to take money or assets out of an IRA, at least as far as the tax rules are concerned. It's possible to get your money tied up in such a way that you can't get your hands on it right away, or you have to incur a surrender charge or other fee, but that would happen only because of a particular investment you chose.

That doesn't mean all distributions can be rolled to another IRA, however. If you've done a rollover within the past 12 months, you can do a direct transfer but not another rollover. Furthermore, you can't move money from one IRA to another in the following situations:

- A required minimum distribution from an IRA can't be rolled to another IRA. The point of the required distribution rules is to force you to take money out of a retirement account, so you can't simply put it back in another one. The original owner of a Roth IRA isn't required to take minimum distributions, however.
- If you inherit an IRA from someone other than your spouse, it appears you can't use a rollover to move money into or out of that IRA.
- If you inherit an IRA from a spouse, you *can* roll money from that IRA to a different one, but in doing so you're electing to treat this as your own IRA. Usually this is not a problem, but if you expect to use the money before age 59½ you may be better off leaving the money in an inherited IRA. The 10% early withdrawal penalty doesn't apply to distributions from an inherited IRA, but it can apply to your own IRA even if all the money came from an IRA you inherited from a spouse.

Whenever you move money from one IRA to another, the recipient IRA has to be the same type (Roth or traditional) unless the move is part of a Roth conversion.

IRA to employer plan. You can't roll a Roth IRA to an employer plan. That's a hard and fast rule, and it applies even if all the money in the Roth IRA came from a rollover from an employer plan.

Employer plans are permitted to accept rollovers from traditional IRAs—but they aren't required to do so. They may refuse because they want to avoid the administrative expense or because of a concern that it's difficult for them to be sure there wasn't a problem of some kind relating to the old account that can potentially taint their plan. Check with your employer to find out what they'll accept before initiating a rollover to their 401k or similar plan. Because the rollover comes from a traditional IRA, it must go to a traditional account in the employer plan, not a Roth account.

If you've made nondeductible contributions to a traditional IRA, the tax rules say you can roll the taxable portion to an employer plan, but you aren't allowed to roll the nontaxable portion. In other words, you can roll an amount representing your deductible contributions and investment earnings, but not the portion representing nondeductible contributions. This rule applies only when rolling to an employer plan: when rolling from one IRA to another, you roll the taxable and nontaxable amounts together.

> Rolling the taxable portion of a traditional IRA to an employer plan leaves you with a traditional IRA that no longer holds any taxable money and can be converted to a Roth without any tax cost. See Chapter 25.

Distributions from employer plans. If you want to move money from an account in an employer plan, the rules are a little different. Perhaps the most important difference is that you aren't allowed to take money from these accounts whenever you want.

Generally you gain access to the money only after a *separation from service*—in other words, when you stop working for the company that maintains the plan. Some companies permit *in-service withdrawals*, or distributions to people who are still working for the company, but subject to restrictions. In particular, regular contributions, whether pre-tax or Roth, can't be paid out to workers who are still employed by the company until they reach age 59½.

Many of these plans allow *hardship distributions*, permitting you to gain access to your account during a financial emergency. You should avoid taking a hardship distribution unless you simply have no other way out of a jam, because the result can be a major setback for your retirement savings. You aren't allowed to roll a hardship distribution to an IRA or to another employer's plan.

Many plans also allow you to borrow money from a 401k or similar account. You aren't allowed to roll this money to another retirement account at the time you take the loan. Certain events, such as a default or separation from service, can result in a *deemed distribution*, where you're treated as if the money you owe on this loan was paid out to you, rather than loaned to you. This type of distribution can be rolled to another retirement account only if the plan where you took the loan makes an *account offset*, reducing your benefit for the amount of the deemed distribution. Information concerning whether a rollover is permitted should be available from that plan.

> Because you already received the money in the form of a loan, you would have to use that money (or other resources) to complete the rollover by transferring cash to a new retirement account. You can't roll the loan itself (that is, the right to receive payments) into an IRA.

As in the case of IRA distributions, you can't roll a required minimum distribution you receive from an employer plan. You also can't roll periodic distributions that are being paid out over your life or for a period of ten years or more, even if these are not required minimum distributions.

And there are other types of distributions that aren't eligible for rollover. You can't roll a distribution that's made to correct an excess contribution, or to satisfy other requirements that apply to the employer's plan. If you receive distributions from the plan that represent dividends on the company's stock or the cost of life insurance, these amounts also are not eligible for rollover.

Indirect rollover to Roth employer account. A special rule applies if you're moving money from a Roth account in one employer plan to a different employer plan. In a direct transfer, you're allowed to move the full amount that was distributed from the old Roth account. If the old plan distributes the money to you, however, a quirk in the rules says you're allowed to roll only the *taxable* portion of the distribution to a different employer's plan.

> **Example:** You change jobs, and your Roth account at the old company has a balance of $14,000, consisting of $11,000 in contributions and $3,000 in investment earnings. The rules permit a direct transfer of the entire $14,000 to a Roth account in your new employer's plan. If the $14,000 is paid out to you, though, only $3,000 can be rolled to a Roth account in your new employer's plan.

This may seem like an awfully peculiar rule. After all, you're rolling money to a Roth account, so a restriction against rolling the nontaxable portion doesn't make a lot of sense. But that's the way the law reads, and the Treasury declined to write a more liberal rule into the regulations.

There's no problem using a rollover to move the entire amount to a Roth IRA, but you need to use a direct transfer if you want to roll an entire Roth account in a 401k or similar plan to another employer's plan.

Tax consequences

Rollovers and direct transfers typically leave you in pretty much the same tax situation as before you made the move. You should be aware of some details, however.

Roth IRA to Roth IRA. Moving money or assets from one Roth IRA to another leaves your tax situation almost entirely unchanged. The starting date of any five-year period remains the same. Likewise, the amount you can withdraw tax-free in a nonqualified distribution is unchanged. The only difference is that if you used a rollover rather than a direct transfer to make this move, you have to wait 12 months before you can do another rollover from one IRA to another (see *One-year waiting period* later in this chapter).

Roth employer account to Roth IRA. You don't report any income when you move money from a Roth account in an employer plan to a Roth IRA, but you don't get to count the time period you held the employer account as part of your Roth IRA holding period. If you already had a time period established for a Roth IRA, you'll continue to use that time period; otherwise you have to start a new time period as of January 1 of the year the money went into your new Roth IRA.

If the money is coming out of the Roth employer account as a qualified distribution, you get to treat the entire amount as basis in the Roth IRA. That means you can withdraw some or all of that amount without reporting any income, even though some of it may represent earnings in the Roth 401k/403b account.

Example: Over the years you contributed $40,000 to your Roth 401k account and the value was $70,000 when you retired. At that time you were over 59½ and the account was more than five years old, so money taken from the account would be a qualified distribution. You decide to roll the entire amount to a Roth IRA.

If this is the first year you had a Roth IRA, you won't be able to take a qualified distribution until January 1 of the fifth year after this occurred. But you can take up to $70,000 in tax-free *nonqualified* distributions from your Roth IRA because the distribution from the Roth 401k account was a qualified distribution.

If the distribution from the Roth 401k account had been a nonqualified distribution (you were under 59½ or the account was less than five years old), you would be allowed only $40,000 in tax-free nonqualified distributions from your Roth IRA.

When you roll only part of a nonqualified distribution from a Roth employer account to a Roth IRA, the taxable part of the distribution is considered to be the first part rolled over. That means you don't have to roll the entire distribution to avoid reporting income.

Example: You receive a distribution of $14,000 from a Roth 401k account, consisting of $11,000 of your contributions and $3,000 of investment earnings. You roll $7,000 to a Roth IRA.

Although you rolled only half the money, you don't report any income. You're treated as having rolled the $3,000 of investment earnings and $4,000 of your contributions. The amount you didn't roll consists entirely of your contributions, so none of that money is taxable.

Roth employer account to new employer plan. Suppose you leave an employer where you had a Roth account and take a job at a different company that has these accounts and accepts rollovers. In this situation you can make a direct transfer from the old employer account to a rollover account in the new employer's plan. Doing so will preserve your basis in the old account (the portion attributable to your after-tax contributions). As noted earlier, if you don't use a direct transfer you can roll only the taxable portion to the new account.

There's another potentially important difference between a rollover and a direct transfer. If you make this move as a direct transfer, you're allowed to count the time you held the old account toward the five years you need for a qualified distribution from the new account. You don't get to count that time if you use a rollover instead of a direct transfer.

How rollovers work

In most cases, a rollover begins with a cash distribution from the old account. The easiest way to complete the rollover is simply to sign the check over to the new trustee. You don't have to do that, though. You can deposit this money in your personal account, and later write a check from that account. In fact, the money you contribute to the new account doesn't have to be the same money you withdrew from the old one. You can spend the money from the old one, and later come up with money from some other source to complete the rollover.

That's almost always a bad idea, though. Whatever you might gain from making temporary use of the money before completing the rollover is almost sure to be much smaller than what you stand to lose if something goes wrong and the rollover isn't completed on time. You're better off keeping this money safe and secure until the rollover is complete.

What's more, when making temporary use of rollover money, there's a chance your actions will be treated as a violation of one of the prohibited transaction rules, such as the rule against borrowing from an IRA. The consequences can be disastrous, including losing bankruptcy protection for your retirement savings.

Rolling assets. It's also possible to roll *assets* (other than money) from one retirement account to another. Normally, if you're moving assets, you would want to use a trustee-to-trustee transfer rather than a rollover, because that would accomplish the move with a single asset transfer rather than two. You're allowed to take assets out of the old account and put them into the new one, though. In fact, you can sell assets you took out of an old IRA and complete the rollover by contributing the sale proceeds to a new IRA.

> **Example:** You hold some weird asset in the old IRA that the trustee doesn't want to sell, or you think you can get a better price if you personally handle the sale. The trustee distributes the asset to you. After that, you can sell the asset and contribute the proceeds to the new IRA, completing the rollover—if you can get this done within 60 days.

Although you can contribute sale proceeds, you *cannot* contribute different assets. You have only two ways to complete a rollover: contribute exactly the same assets you received from the old IRA, or sell those assets and contribute the proceeds of that sale.

Sixty days

To complete a rollover, you have to get the money into the new account within 60 days. Sixty days may seem like plenty of time to complete a rollover after you take money or other assets out of your old account. All too often, though, we see cases where for one reason or another someone failed to complete a rollover on time.

An IRS publication says this time period begins when you receive the distribution. You should play it safe, though. If the check is dated March 12 and you receive it on March 17, make sure you complete the rollover within 60 days after March 12.

> Holding the check without cashing it does not prolong the 60-day period.

Allow for a margin of error on the other end of the transaction. It isn't good enough to mail a check to a new IRA provider within that time period. Your check has to reach them in time to get the money into the new IRA. Don't play it too close!

Missing the deadline. In the bad old days, the 60-day limit was enforced with Procrustean inflexibility. Congress changed the law to give the IRS authority to waive the limit, and the nice people there have been reasonably generous to people who had a good reason for failing to comply. House burned down, serious illness, that kind of thing. They get grumpy, though, and refuse to give relief, if they see that someone was using the rollover rules to obtain a temporary loan from the IRA, or the reason for missing the deadline was mere forgetfulness.

> If the financial institution received your money in time to meet the deadline but the money wasn't credited to your IRA due to their mistake, you may be entitled to automatic relief under a special procedure. Check IRS Publication 590-A for details.

You don't want to get in the position of having to beg for this kind of relief. For one thing, there's a chance the IRS won't think your excuse is good enough. And even if you obtain the relief you're seeking, you're likely to be stuck paying a stiff user fee just to get the IRS to issue a private letter ruling. Remember, you can avoid this issue altogether by doing a trustee-to-trustee transfer instead of a rollover.

Tax consequences of failed rollover. Unless you obtain relief from the IRS, the tax consequences of missing the 60-day deadline can be painful. To begin with, you weren't planning to have a tax bill for this transaction, but now you'll have to report income equal to the taxable portion of the amount withdrawn from the old account. If you're under 59½ years of age, you'll incur the 10% early distribution penalty as well.

> Income from a failed rollover is reported in the year of the distribution, even if the 60-day period expired after the end of the year.

Your tax problems don't end there if you completed the transaction outside the 60-day period. You've put money into a new IRA thinking it would be treated as a rollover contribution, but the rollover rules don't apply. That means it has to be treated as a regular contribution. In many cases the result will be an *excess contribution* because the amount is more than you're allowed to put into the new IRA.

> **Example:** You take $20,000 from an IRA intending to roll it to another IRA, but the rollover isn't completed until 65 days after the distribution. For the year this happened, you're allowed to make $5,000 in regular IRA contributions, and you've actually contributed $3,000.

Because you missed the deadline, you're treated as if you made $23,000 in regular contributions to the IRA ($3,000 in normal contributions and $20,000 from the failed rollover). You were allowed to contribute $5,000, so you have an excess contribution in the amount of $18,000. You'll be faced with a 6% penalty tax on the excess contribution unless you take corrective action as explained in Chapter 20.

> In many cases the worst penalty suffered from a failed rollover is losing the tax benefits associated with keeping the money in a qualified retirement account for years to come.

One-year waiting period

If you make a rollover from one IRA to another, you have to wait a year before making another such rollover. During that year you're allowed to move money or assets from one IRA to another, but only in a direct trustee-to-trustee transfer, not a 60-day rollover.

> A more liberal rule applied before 2015, permitting another rollover without this waiting period, provided that neither of the IRAs involved in the previous rollover (the source IRA or the recipient) was involved in the new rollover.

For purposes of this rule, a rollover from an employer plan is disregarded. Also disregarded is any rollover from a traditional IRA to a Roth (a conversion using a rollover). However, any other rollover from one IRA to another precludes a second one within the following year.

> **Example:** You have two IRAs, a traditional and a Roth. You decide to move half of the Roth IRA to a new account using a rollover. The money is paid out on March 24 and you put it into the new account on April 12.

The one-year period begins on March 24, when the money was paid out. For the next year, you aren't allowed to make another

Roth-to-Roth or traditional-to-traditional rollover. But the following are permitted:

- A rollover from an employer plan,
- A rollover from a traditional IRA to a Roth (a Roth conversion using a rollover), and
- A direct trustee-to-trustee transfer from one IRA to another.

Special situations

The IRS has allowed rollovers that don't necessarily comply with these rules in some special situations. One involves money paid out by certain failed financial institutions. Even if you made a rollover within the previous year, you may be allowed to roll this money into a new IRA because you didn't request this distribution.

Another situation that comes up once in a while is a financial settlement in securities litigation. Someone starts a class action for shareholders of a company and you end up getting some money because your IRA held the stock. The money really belongs to the IRA because that's where you owned the shares. In private letter rulings, the IRS has allowed people to restore these funds to their IRA and treat the transfer as a rollover.

Withholding on plan distributions

Income tax withholding is not required on distributions from IRAs. (You can request income tax withholding on an IRA distribution if you wish.) The general rule for employer plans is different. The employer is required to withhold income tax at the rate of 20% from the taxable portion of the amount distributed to you, even if it's a qualified rollover distribution and you plan to complete a rollover within 60 days. In the case of a traditional account, usually the entire amount is taxable. Even if you have a Roth account, the employer will withhold on the taxable portion, if any. Withholding creates a problem if you intended to roll the entire amount.

> **Example:** You change jobs and take the full amount from a traditional retirement account at the old employer. The account has $50,000, but you receive a check for $40,000 because $10,000 was retained as tax withholding.

You can roll the $40,000 to a new retirement account, but if you do that, you're treated as if you received another $10,000 that wasn't rolled over. You'll have to pay tax on that amount and, if you're under 59½, pay the 10% early distribution penalty as well.

You can avoid that result by depositing $50,000 in the new retirement account within 60 days. In this case you have to come up with $10,000 from another source, though. You can't recover the $10,000 of income tax withholding until you file your tax return for the year this occurred.

A direct transfer eliminates this problem altogether. Your old employer isn't required to withhold income tax when paying out of the retirement plan if the money goes *directly* to an IRA or to an account in your new employer's plan. In the example above, you would simply move $50,000 from one account to another.

Costs of moving your account

Before moving your retirement account you should be aware of costs you may incur. Some may be imposed by the trustee, and some may relate to particular investments.

Account termination. Few IRA providers charge a fee to start an account, because they're eager for your business. Many charge fees for terminating an account, however. The fee may differ depending on the method you use to terminate the account. Some IRA providers charge a hefty fee for handling a direct transfer to a different trustee. They may charge a smaller fee, or none at all, for a regular distribution from the account, even if it's a distribution that terminates the account. As a result, this is one situation where a rollover may be preferable to a direct transfer. Just make sure you follow the rules, because the cost of a failed rollover is almost sure to be a lot more than you can save in fees for a direct transfer.

Asset transfers. If you're transferring assets other than money, such as shares of stock, from one account to another, you may incur additional charges relating to these transfers. Because of the paperwork involved, it's possible both trustees will charge a fee.

Asset sales and purchases. You may be able to avoid asset transfer charges by selling assets in the old account and transferring cash. In that case, though, you may incur brokerage fees and other costs relating to the sale of those assets and the purchase of investments in the new account. Be sure you know about any charges (often called *loads*) imposed in connection with a purchase or sale of mutual fund shares.

Early surrender penalties or charges. If you move money to a new IRA too soon after investing in a certificate of deposit (CD) you may pay a penalty. In most cases the penalty requires you to give up some of the interest you otherwise would have received for the period your money was invested in the CD. That's something you'd like to avoid, but may be the lesser of two evils if you think you'll be much better off in a new investment.

Far more painful in many cases are the surrender charges imposed on annuity purchasers who want out before the end of a stated period typically lasting six to eight years, according to the SEC. If you regret buying an annuity, you may be left with an unpleasant choice between leaving your money in that investment much longer than you'd like or incurring a stiff penalty to move it elsewhere.

Employer plan to IRA

If you receive an eligible rollover distribution from an employer plan you can roll that money to an IRA. A rollover from a traditional account in an employer plan would go to a traditional IRA, and a rollover from a Roth account in an employer plan would go to a Roth IRA. (See Chapter 21 for the rule allowing a direct conversion from a traditional account in an employer plan to a Roth IRA.)

With certain exceptions, you can't take money from an employer plan while still working for that employer. You may have reasons for wanting to move the money to an IRA, but this choice may not be available.

Even when you're in a position to take money from your account, not all distributions are eligible for rollover. You can't roll money you received as a minimum distribution after age 70½ for example. See the discussion earlier in this chapter under the heading *When account moves are possible.*

Differences in tax rules. In some situations it may be helpful to be aware of differences in tax rules between IRAs and employer plans before making a rollover. For example, a special tax treatment is available for certain *lump sum distributions* from employer plans if you were born before January 2, 1936. There's also a special rule allowing capital gain treatment for *net unrealized appreciation* if your distribution includes employer securities (in other words, stock of the company where you worked). These benefits aren't available for IRA distributions, so you should look into them before making your rollover. IRS Publication 575 provides details.

If you're under 59½, you may also want to consider how the 10% penalty applies in each case. The tax law provides a number of exceptions to this penalty, but some apply only when you take money from an employer plan and others apply only when you take money from an IRA.

> **Example:** Your employment terminates in or after the year you reach age 55. If you take money from the former employer's retirement account the 10% penalty doesn't apply. But if you roll the money to an IRA and then take money out before you reach age 59½, you'll incur the penalty unless another exception applies.
>
> **Example:** You receive part of your spouse's retirement account in a divorce. A cash distribution to you from your spouse's account won't be treated as an early distribution because of a special rule for *qualified domestic relations orders* (QDROs). Here again, though, if you roll the money to an IRA you could face the 10% penalty if you tap that account before age 59½.
>
> **Example:** You terminate your employment and decide to go back to school, using part of the retirement account to pay the education expenses. This time it works the other way: you pay the 10% penalty if you use money from an employer plan, but an exception may be available if you roll that money to an IRA and take the money from that account.

Part VI
Taking Money Out

29 Distribution Overview

30 Five-Year Test

31 Exceptions to Age 59½ Test

32 Nonqualified Distributions

33 Liquidating an Account for a Loss

34 Inherited Roth Account

29

Distribution Overview

Here are the main rules that apply when you take money out of a Roth account.

GENERALLY SPEAKING, IT'S DESIRABLE to leave your money in a Roth account as long as possible. The longer your money stays in the account, the more opportunity it has to build up tax-free earnings. Eventually, though, you'll want to take distributions. After all, the point of saving and investing is to have money you can use later.

Access to the money

The tax rules allow you to withdraw from a Roth IRA any time you want. Certain types of investments may limit your access to the money or impose surrender charges or other fees when you take money out. Those are features of the investment you chose, not a requirement of the tax law.

The same is not true for money in a 401k or 403b account. You may be unable to withdraw money from these accounts until after you stop working for the company that maintains the plan. You may be allowed to take a *hardship distribution* or an *in-service withdrawal* under certain circumstances, but you can't always simply pull money out when you want it as you can with an IRA.

> If you have both traditional and Roth accounts in a 401k or similar plan, you may be allowed to choose which type of account the money comes from when you take a withdrawal, but only if your employer has made that choice available.

Required minimum distributions

Tax rules for qualified retirement accounts other than Roth IRAs call for *required minimum distributions* (*RMDs* for short) for each year beginning with the year you reach the age of 70½. You can take your first RMD in the year you reach that age or any time up to April 1 of the following year. All subsequent RMDs have to be made by December 31, and that means you'll have two years' worth of RMDs in a single year if you postpone the first one until after the end of the year you reach age 70½.

> The penalty for failing to take a required minimum distribution is harsh: 50% of the amount by which your actual distribution was smaller than the required amount.

Although you don't have to take RMDs from a Roth IRA, you *do* have to take them from a Roth account in an employer plan. You can avoid having to take those distributions if you roll the employer account into a Roth IRA before the requirement takes effect. If you reach that point without moving your money to a

Roth IRA, a rollover to a Roth IRA will avoid RMDs for future years, but you'll have to take a full year's required minimum distribution for the year of the rollover, and this amount can't be included in the rollover.

> Beneficiaries must take minimum distributions from a Roth IRA after the death of the original owner, as explained in Chapter 34.

Qualified distributions

Distributions from Roth accounts are either qualified or nonqualified. Qualified distributions are entirely tax-free. You can receive these distributions after your account satisfies a five-year requirement and you're at least 59½ years of age. Distributions paid after the death or disability of the original owner can be qualified distributions without regard to the age of the recipient but still must satisfy the five-year requirement. There is also a special rule under which money taken from a Roth IRA and used to purchase a home may be treated as a qualified distribution.

> See Chapter 30 for details of the five-year requirement and Chapter 31 for an explanation of the other requirements.

Nonqualified distributions

Nonqualified distributions can be partly or entirely tax-free as well. The tax treatment depends on whether the distributions come from a Roth IRA or an employer plan.

In the case of a Roth IRA, the first dollars you withdraw are treated as coming from your contributions. These distributions are tax-free, and also free from the 10% penalty for distributions before age 59½. After you've withdrawn all your contributions, the next dollars come from amounts you converted from a traditional account to a Roth IRA. These amounts are also tax-free because you paid tax on these amounts at the time of the conversion. However, if you're under 59½ and the year of the conversion was less than five years ago, you may have to pay the 10% penalty tax. After you've withdrawn your contributions and your conversion money, any additional distributions come from earnings in the account. These amounts are taxable and potentially subject to the 10% penalty. See Chapter 32 for details.

Employer plans. The distribution rules for Roth IRAs don't apply to Roth accounts in employer plans. Instead, the tax treatment of a nonqualified distribution is based on the ratio between your contributions and the total value of the account.

> **Example:** You made contributions of $8,000 to your account. At a time when its current value is $10,000 you withdraw $5,000.

If this is a Roth IRA, you don't report any income on this distribution, and you're left with an account that has $3,000 of contribution money and $2,000 of earnings. If this is an employer account, though, you have to report $1,000 (20% of the $5,000 distribution) as income, because 20% of the total account value represents earnings. You're left with an account that has $4,000 of contribution money and $1,000 of earnings.

Multiple IRAs treated as one

If you have more than one Roth IRA, you're generally required to treat them as a single Roth IRA when you take a distribution. This *aggregation rule* makes it easier to manage your Roth IRAs because you can take money out of the one that's most convenient.

Example: You have one Roth IRA for your regular contributions and another that was created when you did a Roth conversion two years ago. You want to take a withdrawal before age 59½, and you prefer to take this money from the second IRA.

If you withdraw the conversion amount, you may have to pay the 10% penalty because you're under 59½ and the conversion was less than five years ago. But the first dollars you withdraw from *any* Roth IRA will be treated as a return of your contributions. That's true even if you take the money from an IRA where you never made any regular contributions. You can take money from the second IRA without having to pay the penalty so long as the total amount you withdraw is no more than the total amount of your contributions.

The aggregation rule applies to traditional IRAs, too, but separately from Roth IRAs.

Example: You have three traditional IRAs and two Roth IRAs. You may have made nondeductible contributions to one of the traditional IRAs but not the others. When you take money from any of the traditional IRAs you have to add the three of them together to determine the amount of income to report. When you take money from a Roth IRA you have to add the two of them together to determine the tax treatment.

The aggregation rule doesn't apply to Roth accounts in employer plans. Each employer account stands on its own. Also, you don't aggregate inherited IRAs with your own accounts unless you received the account from your spouse and elected to treat it as your own. You can aggregate two accounts you inherited from the same individual, though. (For purposes of the minimum distribution rules, this aggregation is allowed only among inherited accounts that are being distributed under the same life expectancy rule.)

30

Five-Year Test

Your Roth account has to pass a five-year test before you can receive qualified distributions.

THE NORMAL GOAL FOR SAVING IN A ROTH ACCOUNT is to leave the money there until you can take *qualified distributions.* At that point you can take as much money as you like from the account without paying federal income tax. There's no limit on the amount of investment earnings you can withdraw tax-free.

> Nonqualified distributions can also be partly or entirely tax-free, but subject to limitations.

In all cases you have to satisfy two tests to have a qualified distribution. This chapter explains the *five-year test,* which is based on the length of time you've had a Roth account. Details of this test differ depending on whether you have a Roth IRA or a Roth account in an employer plan. The chapter after this one explains exceptions to the *age 59½ test*, which generally requires you to be at least 59½ years of age to receive a qualified distribution. Keep in mind that you need to pass both tests:

- You can pass the five-year test but still have a nonqualified distribution because you're below age 59½ and don't qualify for an exception to the age requirement.
- You can pass the age 59½ test, or qualify for one of the exceptions, but still have a nonqualified distribution because you failed the five-year test.

Contribution trigger

The five-year period starts on January 1 of the first year for which you made a contribution. In a 401k or similar plan, your first contribution to a Roth account might not happen until December. You'll still get credit for the full year, as if the money went in the account on January 1.

> A reemployed veteran may be allowed to contribute to an employer plan for a year of qualified military service that occurred before the year the contribution is made. A contribution to a Roth account that's properly designated to an earlier year when Roth accounts were available starts the five-year period on January 1 of the earlier year for which the contribution was made.

Until April 15 you can make regular contributions to a Roth IRA for the previous year. If you do this, your five-year period starts January 1 of the previous year—the one for which you made the contribution.

Example: You made your first contribution to a Roth IRA on April 10, 2016. If you designated it as a contribution for 2015, your five-year period begins January 1, 2015.

The first day you can take a distribution that satisfies the five-year requirement is January 1 of the fifth year after the year of the first contribution. In the example above, the first contribution relates back to January 1, 2015, so the first day you can take a distribution that satisfies the five-year requirement is January 1, 2020.

Some contributions don't count. According to the tax regulations, a contribution to a Roth IRA won't start the five-year clock running if you later pull it out as a corrective distribution. Presumably the same rule applies if you contribute to a Roth IRA and later recharacterize the transaction as a contribution to a traditional IRA. Similarly, the five-year period for a Roth account in an employer plan doesn't start if a contribution is returned to you for certain reasons.

> **Example:** Before changing jobs you contributed the maximum amount to a traditional 401k account at your old employer. Later that year you started contributing to a Roth 401k account at your new employer, but you withdrew this money from the new account when you realized it would put you over the limit for the year (in other words, it created an *excess deferral*). Because you took the money back as a corrective distribution, this contribution doesn't start the five-year clock.

Similarly, an employer might use an automatic contribution arrangement to put some of your money into a Roth account. You may be able to recover those contributions if you act within 90 days of when they start, but if you do, these amounts won't start the five-year clock.

Conversion trigger

Converting a traditional account to a Roth IRA starts the five-year period as of January 1 of the year of the conversion.

Year-end conversion. In a rollover-type conversion, it's possible to take the money out of a traditional account in one year and contribute it to a Roth IRA in the following year (within 60 days). The five-year period begins the year of the *contribution*, even though the conversion is reported on your tax return for the previous year (the year of the distribution).

In-plan conversion. Subject to various restrictions (see Chapter 21) you may be able to convert a traditional account in a 401k or similar plan to a Roth account within the same plan. Due to an apparent glitch in the legislative language, initially it was unclear whether a conversion would trigger the start of the five-year period for an employer account. The IRS now says an in-plan conversion does trigger the start the clock running, so the safeguard of also making a regular contribution to your Roth account in the employer's plan is no longer necessary.

Five-year rule for multiple Roth accounts

For one reason or another you may have more than one Roth account, either at different times or at the same time. For example, you may move a Roth IRA from one provider to another, or you may maintain two Roth IRAs with different trustees at the same time. You can have a Roth IRA at the same time you have a Roth account in a 401k or similar plan, and if you change jobs you could end up with a Roth account in more than one employer plan. The rules for measuring the five-year period depend on whether we're talking about a Roth IRA or an account in an employer plan.

Roth IRAs. If you have more than one Roth IRA, they're all governed by the same starting date: January 1 of the first year for which you made a contribution to *any* Roth IRA. (See below, however, if you receive distributions from an inherited Roth IRA.)

> **Example:** You started your first Roth IRA in 2011, contributing $1,000. In 2013 you decided to open a new Roth IRA account with a different financial institution. The five-year requirement is satisfied for both accounts as of January 1, 2016.

The result would be the same if you used a rollover or direct transfer to move the old account to a new trustee. It doesn't matter what account we're looking at. The only thing we need to know is the first year for which you made a contribution (including rollover, direct transfer or conversion) to *any* Roth IRA.

Unfortunately, a contribution to a Roth 401k or similar account doesn't start the clock running for a Roth IRA. An IRA doesn't inherit the time from an employer account even if you move the employer account to the IRA in a rollover or direct transfer. This seems like an oversight in the legislation, but nevertheless it's the way the law reads.

In most cases this glitch in the rules will not present a serious problem because you'll be able to take tax-free *nonqualified* distributions from the Roth IRA up to the amount of your basis. (Rules for determining your basis after moving money from a Roth account in an employer plan to a Roth IRA are covered in Chapter 28.) You can eliminate this potential problem altogether, though, if you establish a Roth IRA at the earliest opportunity.

> **Example:** You start saving in a Roth 401k account in 2015. You want to use this account for all your retirement savings, but you set up a Roth IRA the same year with a small contribution, choosing a provider with a low minimum balance and minimal annual fees. If you transfer your Roth 401k account to a Roth IRA at some future date, you'll satisfy the five-year rule as of 2020. That's true even if the transfer is to a different Roth IRA,

because a contribution to one Roth IRA starts the clock running for all Roth IRAs.

The starting date for your first Roth IRA contribution applies even if you're taking money out less than five years after starting the Roth 401k or similar account.

> **Example:** You've had a Roth IRA since 2009, and you start saving in a Roth 403b in 2015. The Roth 403b account won't satisfy the five-year requirement until 2020, but if you roll that account to a Roth IRA you'll meet the test right away because you made your first Roth IRA contribution in 2009. That's true even if the money you're taking from the Roth IRA came from contributions to the 403b plan.

Roth accounts in employer plans. The five-year rule works differently for Roth accounts in a 401k or similar plan. If you establish Roth accounts with more than one employer the five-year requirement has to be satisfied for each account separately.

> **Example:** You start a Roth account with one employer in 2014. Three years later you change jobs, leaving money invested in the old employer's plan but starting a Roth account with the new employer in 2017. You'll satisfy the five-year requirement for the account at the old employer in 2019, but you won't meet the test for the new account until 2022.

There's one exception to this rule. If you make a direct transfer of a Roth account at one employer to a Roth account with a different employer, the starting date for whichever account is older applies after the transfer. This rule does *not* apply if you use a rollover instead of a direct transfer.

Year of distribution

The tax treatment of a distribution is based on when it is actually made, even if it relates to an earlier year.

> **Example:** You reached age 70½ in the year *before* you satisfied the five-year requirement for a Roth 401k account. If you take the required minimum distribution before the end of that year, it will be a nonqualified distribution. You can take this RMD in the following year, though (until April 1), and if you do so it will be a qualified distribution.

Five-year rule after death of account owner

A surviving spouse who is the sole beneficiary of an IRA can elect to treat it as his or her own IRA. In the case of a Roth IRA, this will allow the surviving spouse to use the earliest starting date for any Roth IRA, including the inherited Roth IRA and any Roth IRAs started using his or her own savings.

> **Example:** You started a Roth IRA in 2007 and your spouse started a Roth IRA in 2014. Your spouse died in 2016, leaving you as sole beneficiary of the Roth IRA started in 2014.

If you elect to treat this inherited IRA as your own, you can use the 2007 starting date, so the five-year test is satisfied for both IRAs. The same would be true in the reverse situation, where you started your Roth IRA in 2014 and inherited one started in 2007—but only if you inherit the Roth IRA from a spouse and elect to treat it as your own.

In all other cases (either you are not a surviving spouse or you do not elect to treat the inherited account as your own), you inherit the holding period of the original owner, solely for this account. In the example above, the Roth IRA you started would continue to have its 2004 starting date, but the inherited account wouldn't satisfy the test until 2016.

31

Exceptions to Age 59½ Test

In addition to satisfying the five-year test, you must be at least 59½ to receive a qualified distribution unless an exception applies.

YOU HAVE TO SATISFY TWO TESTS to have a qualified distribution. One is the five-year test explained in the previous chapter. The other test requires you to be at least 59½ years of age at the time of the distribution unless an exception applies. This chapter explains the exceptions to the age 59½ test. Note that these are *not* exceptions to the five-year test. Your account has to satisfy the five-year test even when these exceptions apply.

Exceptions for death and disability apply to all Roth accounts. An additional exception for money used to buy a home is available for Roth IRAs but not for distributions from Roth accounts in employer plans.

Alternate payee

If a distribution goes to a person other than the account owner during the account owner's lifetime, the age of the account owner determines whether the distribution satisfies the age 59½ test.

> **Example:** Pursuant to a divorce decree, at age 56 you receive a distribution from a Roth account owned by your former spouse, who is 62 years of age. This distribution satisfies the age 59½ test.

If you roll the money to your own account, however, you've changed the account owner and the tax treatment of any subsequent distributions will be determined based on your age.

Disability

If your Roth account satisfies the five-year test, you can take qualified distributions before age 59½ if you're disabled, as defined for this purpose. The definition is quite strict:

> An individual shall be considered to be disabled if he is unable to engage in any substantial gainful activity by reason of any medically determinable physical or mental impairment which can be expected to result in death or to be of long-continued and indefinite duration.

A disability that prevents you from earning a living the way you previously did so, but still permits you to perform some kind of work ("substantial gainful activity") doesn't meet the requirement. Likewise, a disability that prevents you from working at all doesn't qualify if it appears to be temporary, as when you're recovering from a serious accident.

> This rule may seem harsh, but remember that even in the case of a nonqualifying distribution, some or all of the money may be tax-free.

Death of the account owner

Distributions to the estate or beneficiaries after the death of the account owner don't have to satisfy the age 59½ test. The age of the original account owner doesn't matter, nor does the age of the beneficiary receiving the distribution. Here again, though, the five-year test continues to apply. See Chapter 34 for more on the death of the account owner.

Distribution used to buy a home

You can take a qualified distribution from a Roth IRA (but not from a Roth account in an employer plan) without being age 59½ if it's a *qualified first-time homebuyer distribution* and your account satisfies the five-year test. Oddly enough, you can be considered a first-time homebuyer even if you previously owned a home, provided you didn't own one within the last two years.

To have a qualified first-time homebuyer distribution, you need to meet all of the following requirements, which are discussed below:

- The purchase must be a principal residence.
- The person for whom it is a principal residence must be the owner of the IRA or a family member (within limits).
- The person for whom it is a principal residence must be a "first-time homebuyer" (generally someone who has not owned a home in the previous two years).
- The purchase must cover qualified acquisition costs.
- The owner of the IRA may not treat more than $10,000 as qualified first-time homebuyer distributions (a lifetime limitation).
- The purchase must be made within the applicable time limit after the distribution.

Principal residence. The qualifying purchase does not have to be a traditional home. For example, a houseboat may qualify for this purpose, if that's your primary home. But the purchase must be a principal residence. It can't be a vacation home where you or your family member stay for a small part of the year.

IRA owner or family member. You can't use this IRA distribution to buy a home for just anyone. It has to be for yourself, your spouse, your child, grandchild or ancestor, or your spouse's child, grandchild or ancestor. If you choose to help a sibling, or a niece or nephew, the rule doesn't apply.

First-time homebuyer. The rule only applies if the person who will use this home as a principal residence is a first-time homebuyer. This is not necessarily someone who has never owned a home, but it must be someone who has not owned a principal residence during the two-year period ending on the date of acquisition of the new home. If that person is married, the spouse must not have owned a principal residence during that period, either.

Qualified acquisition costs. This is a fairly easy requirement to meet. The amounts paid must be costs of acquiring, constructing, or reconstructing a residence, including any usual or reasonable settlement, financing, or other closing costs.

$10,000 limit. This rule is subject to a lifetime limit of $10,000. It appears that this limit applies to the IRA owner, not the purchaser of the home, if these are two different people.

> **Example:** Your son needs $20,000 for the down payment on a home. For this purpose he will take $10,000 from his IRA and you will take $10,000 from your IRA. Assuming neither you nor your son has taken a previous qualified first-time homebuyer distribution, both distributions will qualify.

Example: Your son and daughter each need $10,000 for the down payment on a home. For this purpose you take $20,000 from your IRA. Only the first $10,000 will be a qualified first-time homebuyer distribution.

When you determine whether you are a first-time homebuyer you must take into account any previous ownership of a principal residence by your spouse. But it appears that the $10,000 limit applies separately to each spouse.

Example: You need $20,000 for the down payment on a home. For this purpose you and your spouse each withdraw $10,000 from an IRA. If you meet the other requirements, both distributions can be qualified first-time homebuyer distributions.

It appears that if you are withdrawing from a Roth IRA for this purpose, only the amount of the distribution that exceeds your previous contributions counts toward the $10,000 limit.

Example: You have $14,000 in your Roth IRA, including $8,000 of contributions and $6,000 of earnings. If you meet the other requirements, you can use the entire Roth IRA for the purchase of a principal residence, using only $6,000 of your lifetime limit.

Time limit. Your distribution won't qualify if you take the money out of the IRA too far in advance of the closing of your purchase. The payment must be used to pay qualified acquisition costs before the close of the 120th day after the day on which the payment or distribution is received from the IRA. If you take money out of your IRA and then run into a last minute snag that prevents you from using the money within this time limit, you are permitted to contribute the money back to your IRA (or to a new IRA) within the 120-day limit and treat the distribution and contribution as if you had done a trustee-to-trustee transfer. The 60-day rule that normally applies to rollovers will not apply, and this event is disregarded when you apply the rule that permits only one rollover within a 12-month period.

32

Nonqualified Distributions

Some nonqualified distributions are free of tax, but others may be partly or entirely taxable.

UNLESS YOU'RE DOING A ROLLOVER, if you take a money from a Roth account before it satisfies the five-year test or, subject to the exceptions explained in the previous chapter, before age 59½, you'll have a *nonqualified distribution.* The tax rules for nonqualified distributions from a Roth IRA are somewhat complicated but overall quite favorable, mainly because they allow you to withdraw your contributions tax-free before any of your distributions become taxable. The rules for nonqualified distributions from Roth accounts in employer plans (explained later in this chapter) are completely different.

Treat all Roth IRAs as one

If you have more than one Roth IRA you have to treat them all as a single Roth IRA when applying these rules. It doesn't matter if one of them holds a lot of investment earnings and another has none, or if one of them contains money from a rollover or conversion and another does not. Whenever you take a nonqualified distribution from *any* Roth IRA, it's treated as a distribution from a single IRA that holds all the contribution money, conversion money and investment earnings that are in any Roth IRA you own.

This rule does *not* apply to Roth accounts in employer plans. Each of these accounts stands alone. Also, an inherited Roth IRA is separate from any Roth IRA you started from your own savings unless you inherited the IRA from your spouse and elected to treat it as your own.

How taxable portion is treated

If some or all of your distribution is taxable, that portion will be treated as ordinary income. That's true even if the source was a profit from selling an investment that went up in value while it was held by your IRA. The lower tax rates for long-term capital gain aren't available for this income.

The taxable portion may also be subject to a 10% penalty tax if you receive the distribution before age 59½. This penalty is in addition to the regular income tax. The penalty can also apply to a nontaxable distribution of money from a conversion that occurred less than five years earlier.

Roth IRA, no conversions

Nonqualified distributions from Roth IRAs don't become complicated unless you've done one or more conversions (moving money from a traditional account to a Roth IRA). If you've never done a conversion, all the money in your Roth IRA consists of either contributions or investment earnings. The first dollars taken from the IRA are considered a return of your contributions. This money is tax-free and penalty-free no matter when you take the money.

> Your contributions come out first even if some of the contributions went into the Roth IRA after you started building up investment earnings in the account.

Return of contributions. To know how much money you can withdraw tax-free, you need a running tally of your total contributions over the years. This tally would include all your contributions to all Roth IRAs, except of course any that were removed in corrective distributions or recharacterizations.

Your running total of contributions will be reduced any time you take a distribution from the Roth IRA. At that time you have to file Form 8606, reporting the amount of the distribution and the total amount of your contributions. The IRS will match this information against reports they received from the trustee of your IRA.

Money rolled from employer Roth account. If you move a Roth account from an employer plan to a Roth IRA, amounts you contributed to the employer account count as contributions to the Roth IRA. And if the distribution from the employer account was a qualified distribution (you satisfied the five-year requirement and you were over 59½), your basis in the Roth IRA account (the amount treated as your contributions) includes any earnings in the employer account as of the date of the transfer.

> **Example:** Over a period of several years you contributed a total of $30,000 to a Roth 401k account. After leaving your job at that company you made a direct transfer to a Roth IRA at a time when the total value of the account was $50,000.

If this is the first year you had a Roth IRA, you'll have to wait five years before you can take a qualified distribution from the IRA. But you can take tax-free nonqualified distributions of up to $30,000 from the account. If the distribution from the Roth 401k account was a qualified distribution, you can take up to $50,000 in tax-free nonqualified distributions from the Roth IRA.

Investment earnings. After you've withdrawn all the contributions, any remaining money has to be from earnings on your investments. A nonqualified distribution of the investment earnings will be taxable and, if received before age 59½, potentially subject to the 10% early distribution penalty (see description of exceptions later in this chapter).

Return of conversion money

If you've done one or more conversions, your withdrawal may include a return of some or all the money that went into your Roth IRA in a conversion. The rules here are a little more complicated than we'd like. The main problem is a rule that says the 10% early distribution penalty can apply if you withdraw conversion money before satisfying a five-year test. The five-year test for conversions is distinct from the overall five-year test used to determine whether you've received a qualified distribution. It's possible to take money out after you satisfy the regular five-year test but before you satisfy the separate test for conversions.

> Note however that we're talking about nonqualified distributions. If you satisfy the regular five-year test *and* you're age 59½, your distributions are qualified and you don't have to worry about the separate five-year test for conversion money.

You don't have to pay tax when you take conversion money out of your Roth IRA because you paid tax on those dollars at the time of the conversion. The only issue when you withdraw conversion money is whether the 10% early distribution penalty applies, and if so, does it apply to the entire amount or only to a portion of that money.

Order of distributions. We saw earlier that when you take money from a Roth IRA, your contributions come out before any earnings. When your Roth IRA includes conversion money, those dollars come out *after* your contributions but *before* investment earnings. This rule generally works in your favor:

- First you withdraw your contributions, which are free of tax or penalty.
- Next you withdraw your conversion money, which is free of tax (you paid tax at the time of the conversion) but may be subject to the 10% penalty.
- Last you withdraw investment earnings, which (in a nonqualified distribution) are taxable and potentially subject to the 10% penalty.

We're going to see that there are further ordering rules for the middle slice—the conversion money—because you could be in a situation where the 10% penalty would apply to *some* of your conversion dollars but not all.

The problem. The best way to understand these rules is to see why Congress thought they were necessary in the first place. The law that originally created the Roth IRA didn't have these rules, and the result was a loophole in the rules for the early distribution penalty.

> **Example:** You're under 59½ and want to take money from a traditional IRA. You'll have to pay regular income tax

and, in addition, pay the early distribution penalty because you don't qualify for any of the exceptions.

Without these special rules, you could avoid the 10% penalty by doing a Roth conversion for the amount of money you want to withdraw and, a day or two later, pull the money out of the Roth IRA. This is why Congress imposed a special five-year test for conversion money. They didn't want people to use a Roth conversion as an easy way out of the 10% early distribution penalty.

The five-year test. To prevent this easy avoidance of the 10% penalty, Congress changed the law so that the penalty can apply to a distribution of conversion money that occurs during the five years beginning with the year of a Roth conversion. This is not necessarily the same period used to determine whether you're receiving a qualified distribution.

> **Example:** You made your first contribution to a Roth IRA in 2007, your first conversion in 2012 and another conversion in 2013.

The five-year test used as one of the requirements for a qualified distribution is satisfied on January 1, 2012, because of the contribution you made in 2007. Yet distributions after that date can be nonqualified if you haven't reached age 59½. The 10% penalty can apply to a nonqualified distribution of money from the 2012 conversion until 2017, and money from the 2013 conversion until 2018.

No additional penalty. Congress was trying to protect the existing penalty, not create an additional penalty. That means you won't have to pay the penalty in a situation where it wouldn't apply to a distribution from a traditional IRA.

> **Example:** You created your first Roth IRA with a conversion at age 58, and took a distribution at age 60.

This is a nonqualified distribution because you haven't satisfied the regular five-year test. You also haven't satisfied the special five-year test that applies to conversions, but that doesn't matter. This test is used only to determine whether the early distribution penalty applies. You've reached the age of 59½, so the penalty doesn't apply in any event.

Multiple conversions. If you've done more than one Roth conversion, it can make a difference *which* conversion is the source of your distribution. The regulations say you're treated as taking money from the earliest conversion first, then the next one and so on. You can't take money from a later conversion before exhausting an earlier one, even if that choice would produce a better result.

> **Example:** You did a $10,000 Roth conversion four years ago and another $10,000 Roth conversion two years ago. Now you're taking a $10,000 distribution that comes from conversion money.

Both conversions fail the five-year test, so the 10% penalty may apply either way. Because you're paying the penalty now in any event, you might prefer to take money from the second conversion. That way you would continue to have money in the Roth IRA that was converted four years ago, so you can satisfy the five-year test if you take another distribution a year later. You aren't allowed to do that, though. Your distributions come from the earliest conversion until all that money has been distributed.

> This is true even if the conversions are in separate Roth IRAs and the distribution comes from the one used for the later conversion. You have to treat all your Roth IRAs as a single Roth IRA for this purpose.

Converted IRA has basis. There's one more tricky aspect to distributions of conversion money. If you made nondeductible contributions to your traditional IRA, those contributions created *basis*, and that means part of your conversion was tax-free. You don't have to pay the 10% penalty when you take tax-free money from a traditional IRA, so the rules say the penalty doesn't apply if you convert this money and later pull it out of the Roth IRA.

> **Example:** You made a total of $7,000 in nondeductible contributions to your traditional IRA over a period of several years, and converted it to a Roth IRA when the value was $10,000. Less than five years later you withdrew this money from the Roth IRA.

At the time of the conversion you paid tax on $3,000, because you had $7,000 of basis in your traditional IRA. If you had simply withdrawn the $10,000 from the traditional IRA, the 10% penalty would have applied only to the $3,000 taxable amount. That means the penalty applies only to $3,000 of the distribution you took from the Roth IRA.

In the example above you took the entire $10,000 conversion amount from the Roth IRA, so it's clear enough that you received $7,000 free and clear and $3,000 that's potentially subject to the 10% penalty. What if you took only a portion of the conversion amount from the Roth IRA?

> **Example:** The facts are the same as in the previous example, except you withdrew $4,000 of the conversion money and left the other $6,000 in your Roth IRA.

This is one area where the Treasury adopted a rule that's unfavorable and not particularly logical. The regulations say that when you take conversion money from a Roth IRA, and the conversion was only partly taxable, the first dollars come from the taxable part of the conversion. You don't get to withdraw money from the nontaxable part of the conversion until you've taken out all the taxable money. In the example above, your $4,000 distribution would include $3,000 of money from the taxable part of the conversion and only $1,000 from the nontaxable part. That means you could get stuck paying the 10% penalty on the entire $3,000, even though you took out less than half the conversion money.

Multiple conversions with basis. We saw earlier that if you do more than one conversion, any distribution of conversion money will come first from the earliest conversion. This rule continues to apply when you're converting from a traditional IRA that has basis. As a result, withdrawals of conversion money that occur after multiple conversions can alternate between amounts that are potentially subject to the 10% penalty and amounts that are not.

> **Example:** You convert $10,000 from a traditional IRA in which 70% of the money is basis from nondeductible contributions and 30% is investment earnings. A year later you convert another $10,000 from your traditional IRA. At this point 60% of the money is from nondeductible contributions.

If you take nonqualified distributions from your Roth IRA, the first $3,000 is from the taxable portion of the first conversion (potentially subject to the 10% penalty); the next $7,000 is from the nontaxable portion of the first conversion (penalty-free); the next $4,000 is from the taxable portion of the second conversion (potential penalty); and the next $6,000 would be from the nontaxable portion of the second conversion.

Reminder. When we talk about the taxable portion of the conversion, we're referring to the part that was taxable *at the time of the conversion*. This money isn't taxed again when you take it out of your Roth IRA, but it's potentially subject to the 10% early distribution penalty. You don't have a taxable distribution from your Roth IRA until you take investment earnings, and that happens only after you've withdrawn all your contributions *and* all your conversion money.

Distributions from Roth employer accounts

It might seem logical that nonqualified distributions from Roth accounts in 401k or other employer plans would be treated like nonqualified distributions from Roth IRAs. Not even close. The two sets of rules are completely different. We have to consider two different issues: how much of the distribution will be treated as earnings (and therefore taxable), and how much of the nontaxable portion will be treated as coming from conversion money (and therefore potentially subject to the 10% penalty tax on retirement plan distributions received before age 59½).

Taxable portion. The rule for figuring the taxable portion is relatively simple, though less favorable than the rule for IRAs. You determine what portion of the total account consists of investment earnings (rather than contributions or conversion money) and apply that percentage to the distribution.

> **Example:** You withdraw $5,000 from your Roth 403b account at a time when its value is $20,000, consisting of $14,000 in contributions and $6,000 in investment earnings.

You have to treat $1,500 (30% of your distribution) as a distribution of earnings because earnings represent 30% of the overall value of the account. After the distribution, you're treated as owning an account that has $10,500 in contributions, because you withdrew $3,500 of your contributions when you took $5,000 from the account.

Notice that you get a different result if you roll the Roth 403b account to a Roth IRA and then take $5,000 from the Roth IRA. The rollover would create a Roth IRA that has $14,000 in contributions and $6,000 in basis, the same as the Roth 403b account, but now if you take $5,000 from the Roth IRA, the first dollars come from your contributions. A rollover isn't always possible, though. For example, if you take money from an employer plan Roth account in a hardship distribution, you aren't allowed to roll that money to a Roth IRA, so the rule described here will determine the amount of investment earnings included in the distribution.

The amount of investment earnings in your account is determined in relation to the overall account value. That's true even if some of the value represents unrealized appreciation—in other words, stocks or other assets that went up in value and haven't been sold. What's more, the calculation will be based on the overall account, combining the part that represents your contributions with the part that represents an in-plan conversion if both of these apply, even if you're withdrawing money only from one side (conversion money or contribution money). You won't have to do this calculation: the company maintaining the plan will determine the amount that's taxable and give you a copy of the report they send to the IRS.

> Remember, when we're talking about employer plans, your Roth accounts at each employer stand alone. If you have Roth accounts with more than one employer, you won't treat them as a single account the way you would if you had more than one Roth IRA.

Conversion portion. Here's where things get strange. Recall that you can get hit with a 10% early distribution penalty on the *nontaxable* portion of a distribution if it relates to a conversion less than five years earlier. This rule applies to Roth accounts in employer plans as well as Roth IRAs, so if you take a nonqualified distribution from a Roth account in a 401k or similar plan we need to know whether the nontaxable portion came from your contributions (which would be free from the early distribution penalty) or from your in-plan conversion (which could be hit with the penalty if the conversion was less than five years before the distribution).

The way this rule fits with the rule for determining the taxable portion—or fails to fit, I should say—reminds me of a piano piece I once heard where the left hand plays in one key and the right hand plays in a different one. Here's why. If your account is divided between contribution money and money from an in-plan conversion, you add everything together when figuring how much is taxable (as stated above). But we treat these two components separately to determine whether the nontaxable portion came from contributions or a conversion.

The general rule is that the nontaxable portion comes first from contributions until the total amount of nontaxable distributions is equal to the total amount of your contributions. After that, any additional nontaxable distributions come from conversion money (potentially subject to the penalty). This is similar to the rule for Roth IRAs. But there's a twist.

You could be in a situation where you're eligible to take a distribution from the conversion portion of your account but not from the contribution portion of your account. This might happen when you're still employed with the company and under age 59½, but the conversion portion of the account isn't subject to this restriction. (The conversion portion would be restricted if it came from your contributions to a traditional 401k account, but might not be restricted if it came from a different source, such as profit-sharing contributions made by your employer.)

So here's the rule. If the only portion of the account available for distributions is the conversion portion, then the nontaxable portion of your distribution is treated as coming first from conversion money, potentially subject to the penalty, even though you haven't withdrawn your contributions.

Playing in different keys. Here's an example to show what I mean about two hands playing in different keys. Suppose your Roth account contains $20,000 in contributions, which have produced $0 earnings, and a $14,000 conversion, which has produced $6,000 in earnings. Overall, your account is worth $40,000, which consists of $34,000 in after-tax money and $6,000 in pre-tax money. Within five years after the conversion, you take a nonqualified distribution of $20,000 at a time when you're allowed to withdraw from the conversion money (including earnings) but not the contribution money.

First we have to determine how much of the distribution is taxable. We look at the overall account value of $40,000 and see that 85% is after-tax money, so 15% of the $20,000 distribution, or $3,000, is taxable. That means $17,000 of the distribution comes from after-tax dollars. The distribution is coming from the conversion side of your account, where you have only $14,000 of basis. Now what?

You'll still have to treat only $3,000 as taxable. The distribution comes from conversion money, so the non-taxable portion comes first from the conversion, making it potentially subject to the 10% penalty. Yet you have only $14,000 in after-tax conversion money, so this 10% penalty is limited to that amount.

You withdrew $20,000, all from the conversion money and earnings on that money. Of this amount, $3,000 is taxable (and potentially subject to the 10% penalty). Another $14,000 is from the original conversion amount, before the earnings, and the 10%

penalty may apply to this amount also because the conversion occurred less than five years earlier. You also received another $3,000 that was treated as nontaxable, because we look at the entire account, not just the conversion side, when determining the taxable amount. This portion escapes the 10% penalty because you've already paid the penalty on the taxable amount plus the entire $14,000 conversion amount.

What happens to this amount? It's free of tax and penalty, so you're treated as if you received it from the contribution side. Now you're going to be treated as if you have $17,000 of basis and $3,000 of earnings left in your account, even though you withdrew all the money from the conversion side, which is where all the earnings were, and you still have $20,000 on the contribution side of your account. You end up paying tax and penalty on the proper amounts, but to get there we have to act as if some of your contribution money was swapped over to the conversion side of your account in exchange for earnings.

> At times like this I feel compelled to point out that I didn't write these rules.

Exceptions to the 10% penalty

You may be hit with a 10% early distribution penalty if you take a nonqualified distribution from a Roth account. It doesn't apply to the portion of your distribution that comes from contributions, but it can apply to investment earnings, and in some cases to conversion money. The idea behind this penalty is to encourage you to leave money in your retirement account until you reach retirement age, which for this purpose is arbitrarily set at 59½.

Despite this policy, Congress has recognized that you may have to tap a retirement account before reaching that age in a number of situations and provided various exceptions. As you review the list, note that some of them apply only to IRA distributions and some apply only to money that comes from employer plans.

Exceptions that apply to particular types of expenses do not require you to use money from your retirement account for the direct payment of that expense. For example, if you have a medical expense that qualifies for the exception listed below, you can pay that expense from your regular checking account and take a later distribution from your IRA. The exception will still apply if the distribution occurred in the same year you paid the medical expense.

> The following list doesn't provide full details for all the exceptions. Further information may be found in IRS Publication 590-B (for IRAs) or 575 (for employer plans).

Death of account owner. The 10% penalty doesn't apply to money you receive as beneficiary after the death of the original account owner. This exception applies to IRAs and also to accounts in 401k and other employer plans. You lose the benefit of this exception, however, if you're a surviving spouse and you roll the account into one that you own, or you elect to treat the decedent's account as your own.

Disability. The penalty doesn't apply to money you receive after you become disabled, under the same strict definition discussed in Chapter 31. This exception applies to IRAs and also to accounts in employer plans.

Periodic payments. Money received from a retirement account (IRA or employer plan) in the form of substantially equal periodic payments according to an IRS-approved method escape the early distribution penalty. You have to adhere strictly to the chosen method until age 59½ or for a period of five years, *whichever is* *later*, or the penalty may apply retroactively. Technical details of this exception are beyond the scope of this book, so you should see a professional with expertise in this area if you want to pursue this choice.

> Unscrupulous advisors have pushed some people into using this method to take money from retirement accounts and make new investments with the advisor. The advisor benefits from a sales commission but the customer would be better off leaving the money in the retirement account.

Disaster areas. Residents of various disaster areas may qualify for tax-favored withdrawals and repayments and, in the case of 401k or 403b plans, relaxed rules for plan loans. See IRS publications in the 4492 series for details.

Medical expense. You can avoid the 10% penalty if you paid medical expenses the same year as your distribution from a retirement account (IRA or employer plan), but only to the extent you would be able to claim an itemized deduction for the expenses. This means your qualified expenses must exceed a percentage of your adjusted gross income (10% unless you're over 65, in which case 7.5% for now but 10% beginning in 2017). You don't have to itemize to use this exception, but only the portion of the expenses meeting this standard will excuse you from the penalty.

Divorce. Procedures here differ depending on whether the money comes from an employer plan or an IRA. In the case of an employer plan, the 10% penalty doesn't apply to a distribution made to an alternate payee pursuant to a *qualified domestic relations order* (QDRO). This exception doesn't apply to IRAs, but the tax law allows a transfer of an interest in an IRA as part of a divorce, with no tax being paid and the transferee being treated as the new owner.

Qualified reservist distributions. The 10% penalty doesn't apply to *qualified reservist distributions* from a retirement account (IRA or employer plan). Requirements include being called to active duty after September 11, 2001 for a period of more than 179 days or for an indefinite period, and taking a distribution no earlier than the call to active duty and no later than the close of the active duty period.

IRS levy. The penalty doesn't apply to distributions made because of an IRS levy against your retirement account (IRA or employer account).

Health insurance for unemployed. If you receive unemployment compensation for twelve consecutive weeks you may be able to receive penalty-free distributions from an IRA (but not from an employer plan) to the extent of health insurance costs for yourself, your spouse and your dependents.

College costs. An exception for distributions from IRAs (but not from an employer plan) may apply if you pay college costs for yourself or your spouse, or for children or grandchildren of yourself or your spouse.

Distribution to buy a home. The rules described in Chapter 31 as a way to have a qualified distribution when buying a home can also be used to avoid the 10% penalty on a taxable distribution from an IRA (but not from an employer plan). For example, a distribution from a Roth IRA that's less than five years old would not be a qualified distribution, but the 10% penalty wouldn't apply to the taxable portion of the distribution if you satisfy the home purchase requirement.

Separation from service. If your employment terminates in or after the year you turn 55, you can avoid the 10% penalty on distributions from an employer plan (but not from an IRA).

33

Liquidating an Account for a Loss

If your Roth account has lost value, you may gain a tax benefit from liquidating it.

IF YOU'VE LOST MONEY IN YOUR ROTH IRA, you're not alone. Even the best investors sometimes get caught in a downdraft, and when the stock market heads south there's plenty of pain to go around.

If your Roth loses money shortly after you converted from a traditional IRA, your best choice is probably to undo the conversion. After waiting long enough you can convert again. Usually the lower value of the account means you'll pay a smaller tax on the second conversion. But what if it's too late to undo the conversion?

Loss on liquidation

Ordinarily, distributions from a traditional IRA are taxable, so the tax "benefit" when your account loses value is that you report a reduced amount of income rather than claiming a loss deduction. Yet if you've made nondeductible contributions to a traditional IRA, you recover those contributions—your IRA's "basis"—free of tax. If your account ends up with a value smaller than its basis, the IRS allows a deduction, but only if you completely liquidate all your traditional IRAs.

For technical reasons, it wasn't always clear that this deduction is available for Roth IRAs. Since 2001, though, the IRS gives a favorable answer in the relevant publication (now Publication 590-B): if you liquidate all your Roth IRAs for an amount that's less than your basis, you can claim a deduction for your loss. Your basis is the amount of your contributions to the Roth, including conversion contributions, reduced by any amounts you've withdrawn.

What kind of deduction?

You might expect to get a capital loss deduction in this situation. After all, in most cases the IRA lost value because stocks, mutual funds or other investments in the IRA declined. Instead, the IRS says this is a miscellaneous itemized deduction that's subject to the 2% floor. Here's what that means.

On the good side, this is an "ordinary" deduction rather than a capital loss. That means the $3,000 capital loss limitation doesn't apply, and the deduction counts against income that's taxed at the highest rate that applies to you.

There's a drawback, though. The deduction is available only if you itemize. If you normally claim the standard deduction, it may pay to consider itemizing to claim your IRA loss. But if your loss isn't big enough, you might still be better off with the standard deduction, and that means you get no benefit from liquidating your IRA.

And there's another drawback: the 2% floor. All your deductions that fall into this category of "miscellaneous" itemized deductions get lumped together and reduced by 2% of your adjusted gross income (AGI). If you don't have other miscellaneous deductions, the entire 2% reduction comes out of your IRA deduction.

> **Example:** You converted a traditional IRA when it was worth $5,000 and now it's worth $1,500. Your AGI is $90,000. If you liquidate the Roth for a loss of $3,500, you'll have to reduce that amount by $1,800 (2% of your AGI), leaving you with a deduction of only $1,700.

And there's another drawback. Miscellaneous deductions aren't allowed for purposes of the alternative minimum tax (AMT). That means you could lose the benefit of the deduction (or some of the benefit) because of the AMT rules. This type of AMT situation doesn't give rise to an AMT credit you can recover in future years, so any part of the deduction that gets swallowed up in the AMT is lost forever.

Liquidating your IRA

To qualify for the deduction for losses in a Roth IRA, you have to liquidate all your Roth IRAs. You can't claim a loss on one Roth while keeping another Roth in place, even if all the loss occurred in one Roth. The same rule applies to traditional IRAs where the value is less than your basis. However, you don't have to liquidate traditional IRAs to claim your loss in a Roth, or vice versa.

Bear in mind that if you converted from a traditional IRA, liquidation of your Roth will result in a penalty equal to 10% of the distribution if you're under 59½ and the distribution occurs before the fifth year after the conversion. If your account still has substantial value, you may want to delay liquidation of a conversion Roth IRA even though this will delay your deduction. You don't have to worry about this if your Roth has only annual (non-conversion) contributions because the penalty for that type of Roth applies only to earnings. A Roth isn't considered to have earnings if the overall value has decreased, even if the Roth received amounts like interest and dividends that would normally be considered earnings.

Is it worth it?

Whether it makes sense to liquidate your Roth to claim this deduction depends on many factors. Do you itemize? How large is the loss compared with 2% of your AGI? How much do you lose by removing what's left of your account from the Roth IRA, where it has the potential to produce tax-exempt earnings? Will you incur a 10% penalty if you liquidate now? This can be a complicated decision, so you may want to consult with a tax professional before making this move.

34

Inherited Roth Account

Rules for distributions from an inherited Roth account.

WE SOMETIMES SEE STATEMENTS LIKE THIS: "On your death, your beneficiaries receive your Roth IRA tax-free." That statement could be a little misleading. For one thing, the estate tax applies to assets you own in a Roth IRA the same way it applies to assets you own in a traditional IRA. What's more, if you die less than five years after setting up a Roth IRA, your beneficiaries may have to pay tax on earnings if they withdraw them too soon.

Estate tax

The federal estate tax applies to assets you own at death if your taxable estate is above an exemption amount, set at $5,430,000 as of 2015. Roth IRAs don't enjoy any special exemption from the estate tax. If you own a Roth IRA at death and it passes to someone other than your spouse, it will be included in your taxable estate.

There is one way Roth IRAs provide an estate tax benefit. Your annual and conversion contributions to a Roth IRA are paid with after-tax dollars. That means the size of your estate has been reduced by the amount of tax you paid on those dollars. The result is that you have a smaller estate even though the value of what you're passing to your beneficiaries is no smaller than if you had a traditional IRA. That's why you may hear people say you receive estate tax savings from a Roth IRA. The estate tax savings come from the fact that you've already paid the income tax, not from any special estate tax rule that applies to Roth IRAs.

> The estate tax savings from a Roth conversion may not be as great as they appear due to an itemized deduction that can be claimed by beneficiaries receiving taxable distributions from retirement accounts that were subjected to estate tax (so-called *income in respect of a decedent*, or *IRD*). For various reasons, the IRD estate tax deduction may not fully eliminate the double tax on inherited IRAs, so a conversion may produce estate tax savings despite the availability of this deduction.

Income tax

The income tax treatment of a Roth account following death is the same as before death, with three exceptions:

- The 10% early distribution penalty generally does not apply to post-death distributions, although it can apply to a spouse who elects to treat a Roth IRA as his or her own Roth IRA.
- Beneficiaries can withdraw earnings tax-free, even if the beneficiary is under 59½ and the decedent was under 59½—but only if the five-year requirement is satisfied.

- Beneficiaries may be required to take distributions according to rules described below.

One rule that does not change is the requirement for the Roth IRA to exist at least five years before earnings can be withdrawn tax-free. To be more precise, earnings can be withdrawn tax-free beginning on the first day of the fifth taxable year after the year the first Roth IRA was established.

As a result, a beneficiary may have to pay tax on earnings withdrawals if the original owner's death and the beneficiary's withdrawal both occur shortly after the Roth IRA is established. This result isn't as harsh as it may seem, however. The tax only applies to earnings that built up after the contribution to the Roth IRA. Normally that's a small portion of the Roth IRA if the withdrawal occurs just a short time after the original owner established the Roth IRA. What's more, a beneficiary can avoid this tax by leaving the earnings in the Roth IRA for the required amount of time—even if the beneficiary immediately withdraws everything except the earnings.

> **Example:** In 2015 you inherit a Roth IRA that was established by a conversion in 2013. The Roth IRA includes $96,000 from the conversion contribution and $4,000 of earnings. You can immediately withdraw the entire $100,000 and pay tax (but no penalty) on the $4,000 of earnings. Or you can withdraw up to $96,000 (paying no tax or penalty) and leave the $4,000 of earnings in the Roth IRA until 2018, when you can withdraw the balance of the Roth IRA tax-free.

Non-spouse beneficiary of Roth IRA

If you inherit a Roth IRA from someone other than your spouse, you aren't permitted to make contributions to the inherited IRA or combine it with any Roth IRA you established for yourself.

What's more, you have to follow the minimum distribution rules for inherited IRAs.

When you inherit a traditional IRA, the distribution rules depend on whether death occurred before the required beginning date for distributions. There's no required beginning date for distributions from a Roth IRA, so they're always subject to the rules for death occurring before the required beginning date.

For a beneficiary other than a spouse, distributions must satisfy one of the following rules:

- *Rule 1:* Receive the entire distribution by December 31 of the fifth year following the year of the owner's death.
- *Rule 2:* Receive the entire distribution over your life, or over a period not extending beyond your life.

The original owner may have specified which rule applies in the document used to set up the Roth IRA. More often, the choice is left to the beneficiary. If the choice is yours, you have to choose by December 31 of the year following the year the death occurred, because that's the last day to start receiving distributions under Rule 2.

Suppose you choose Rule 1. In this case you can delay your distribution, if necessary, until the fifth year after the year the IRA was established, to avoid paying tax on distributions of earnings. You can also withdraw all amounts other than earnings before that time without paying tax or penalty. When you reach January 1 of the fifth year after the year the original owner established the Roth IRA, you can withdraw the earnings as well without any tax or penalty.

If you choose Rule 2 instead, you may be required to take some distributions before the Roth IRA has existed five years. That's unlikely to be a problem though, because you're not considered to have withdrawn any earnings until after you withdraw all the contributions (including conversion contributions). The required distributions under this rule are a small percentage of the overall value of the Roth IRA, so you probably won't take any distributions of earnings within five years unless you withdraw more than the required amount.

> The Obama administration has floated a proposal to do away with Rule 2, so that non-spouse beneficiaries would be required, with some exceptions, to withdraw the entire account within five years after the death of the owner from whom they inherited.

Spouse beneficiary of Roth IRA

If you inherit a Roth IRA from your spouse you can elect to treat it as your own IRA. That means you can make regular or conversion contributions to this IRA, assuming you are otherwise eligible to make such contributions to a Roth IRA of your own. Furthermore, the required distributions described above don't apply to a Roth IRA you elect to treat as your own. You can leave the money in the IRA as long as you want. Note, however, that if you elect to treat the Roth IRA you inherit from your spouse as your own IRA, all the rules apply as if you started the IRA. In particular, you may not be able to withdraw earnings free of tax or penalty until you reach age 59½.

> If you don't elect to treat the IRA as your own, it's treated the same as if inherited by a non-spouse beneficiary as described above.

Index

age 59½
  alternate payee 269
age limit 84
alimony income 92
annuities
  valuation 204
banks 78
beneficiaries 80
brokerage commissions 199
college costs 290
college savings 68
combat pay
  qualifying income 93
contributions
  age limit 84
  and employer plan 85
  deadline 83
  hurricane 86
  income limitation *Chapter 15*
  married filing separately 85
  military death benefits 86
  minimum age 84
  multiple IRAs 85
  other savings 83
  other than cash 86
  overlap period 84
  overview 18
  qualifying income *Chapter 14*
  repayment 86
  reservist 86
  to conversion Roth IRA 85
  traditional IRA 85
  troubleshooting *Chapter 20*
  year of conversion 85
conversion
  12-month rule 147
  advanced strategies *Chapter 25*
  after recharacterization 151
  amount converted 156
  amount taxable 156
  consequences *Chapter 22*
  deadline 145
  decision *Chapter 10*
  eligibility 145
  employer account 158
  estimated tax 161
  filing status 146
  general rules *Chapter 21*
  hidden benefit 63
  in retirement 64
  methods 144
  no penalty 161
  ordinary income 161
  overview 19
  partial 148
  periodic payments 149
  recharacterizing *Chapter 23*
  separate IRA 187
  source of tax money 150
  strategies *Chapters 24 and 25*
  tax bracket 176
  tax payment 181
  timing 179
  undoing and redoing 171, 180
  vs rollover 143
  when in doubt 175
  year taxable 160
corrective distribution 132
death of account owner 270
differential wage payments 93
disability 269
distributions
  access to money 255
  minimum required 256
  multiple IRAs 258
  nonqualified 257
  overview *Chapter 27*
  qualified 257

diversification 213
divorce 289
early distribution penalty 49
    exceptions 287
effective size of account *Chapter 6*
employer account
    access 56
    eligibility 53
    expenses 55
    investments 54
Employer plans
    Roth contributions *Chapter 17*
estate tax 295
excess contribution
    later year less than maximum 135
excess contributions
    401k/403b 135
    correcting 131
    IRA 130
fees 79
first-time homebuyer
    $10,000 limit 271
    120-day limit 272
    family member 271
    previous homeowner 271
    principal residence 271
    qualified acquisition costs 271
    requirements 270
five-year test *Chapter 28*
    death of account owner 266
    multiple accounts 263
    when period begins 261
    year of distribution 266
hardship withdrawals 56
health insurance 290
home purchase 70, 270, 290
hurricane relief 86, 289
imagine *Chapter 3*
income limitation
    exceeding 102
    filing status 98
    proportionate reduction 101
    special rules 102
income within account 197
inherited account *Chapter 34*
inherited Roth IRA
    income tax 296
    non-spouse beneficiary 297
    spouse beneficiary 299
insurance companies 79
investing *Chapter 27*
    managed funds 224
investing style 78
investment expenses 198
investments
    account allocation 231
    annuities 226
    asset allocation 210
    bad ideas 227
    bonds 207
    CDs 207
    company stock 219
    diversification 213
    expenses 218
    index funds 221
    key principles 208
    money markets 207
    other 208
    overview 20
    prohibited 200
    real estate 208
    risk 213
    saving 209
    simple approach 229
    stable value funds 207
    stocks 207, 211
    types 207
IRA providers 78–79
    banks 78
    fees 79
    insurance companies 79
    mutual funds 78
    stock brokers 78
IRA used as security 202
keeping records 80
legislative changes 12
liquidating account *Chapter 33*
    itemized deduction 292
    loss 292
marginal tax rate 44
matching contributions 54
medical expense 289
military death benefits 86
minimum required distributions 256
modified AGI
    adjusted gross income 99
    capital gains 100
    estimating AGI 76
    modifications 100
multiple IRAs 258
mutual funds 78
nonqualified distributions *Chapter 32*
    conversion money 277
    multiple IRAs 274

Roth IRA 275
taxable portion 275
other investments 77
parity principle *Chapter 5*
personal use property 203
plan loans 56
prohibited investments 200
prohibited transactions 201
qualifying income *Chapter 14*
alimony 92
combat pay 93
differential wage payments 93
employee earnings 89
foreign income 89
household chores 94
items excluded 89
parent's business 95
safe harbor 89
self-employment income *See* self-employment income
spouse's income 92
rate shifting 62, *Chapter 8*
recharacterization 131
after transfer 128, 171
consequences 127
contributions *Chapter 19*
deadline 124, 167
defined 164
extended deadline 125, 167
investment performance 126, 169
not allowed 123
procedure 121, 164
super-extended 168
timing 124, 167
uses 122
recharacterizations
overview 20
record keeping 80
related person transactions 201
required minimum distributions 41, 61
reservists 86, 290
retirement megatrends 13
retirement savings credit *Chapter 18*
distributions 118
eligible contributions 117
income limits 116
minors, students 116
nonrefundable 119
rollovers *Chapter 26*
costs 249
direct transfer compared 235
employer plan to IRA 251
failed 246
importance 235
mechanics 243
one-year rule 247
overview 21
sixty-day rule 244
special situations 248
tax consequences 241
when possible 236
withholding 248
Roth 401k/403b
availability 110
contribution limit 111
contributions *Chapter 16*
designating contributions 111
matching contributions 113
participation 110
Roth 401k/403b distributions
overview 22
Roth IRA
contribution limit 82
eligibility 81
establishing 80
for minor 79
small 77
starting 75
Roth IRA distributions
overview 21
self-employment income 90
active involvement 90
investment income 91
kinds 90
losses 91
net earnings 91
S corporations 91
SEP IRA 83
services provided to IRA 203
SIMPLE IRA 83
sixty-day rule 244
social security
taxation of benefits 61
social security benefits 48
spousal IRA
who contributes 93
spousal Roth IRA
joint IRA 85
stock brokers 78
tax brackets 38
tax savings preservation fallacy *Chapter 4*
time advantage *Chapter 7*
time frame 77

transactions with IRA 202
trustee fees 199
unrelated income 198
value shifting 205
wash sales 203
wrap fees 199

16927079R00169

Printed in Great Britain
by Amazon